PRA

JAGUARS AND CANNIBALS

"It has been my privilege to be friends with Wayne for the last twenty-five years. He is an incredible individual who has lived a life that most of us only dream of. Fortunately for us, Wayne has taken the time to write his life's journey for us to live and enjoy. This book is a collection of experiences that cannot be duplicated. By reading them, you will be taken with Wayne, living the moments as he vividly describes each venture in real-time action. We have experienced incredible scenarios together in numerous world locations. I have often said to myself that if I had not been there in person, it would be very difficult for me to assimilate, believe, and enjoy the moments."

Allan Pratt, physician and farmer

"I have known Wayne for quite a long time, and have always enjoyed talking to him about our common interest in the great country of Brazil and specifically the great Amazon basin. Wayne personifies a statement made by my friend's son, when he said, "Dad, you and Mom are sucking the very marrow out of the bones of life." Certainly, Wayne fits this description. His stories are fascinating and insightful and I have enjoyed reading about his amazing adventures."

Gary Neeleman, Honorary Consul of Brazil
co-author of *Tracks in the Amazon* and *The Rubber Soldiers*

"Wayne is a great writer and an adventurous soul. He has many things to teach about life and the excitement of the world around us."

Dale T. Tingey, PhD
American Indian Services

JAGUARS AND CANNIBALS

TRUE STORIES OF AN LDS TREASURE HUNTER

JAGUARS AND CANNIBALS

TRUE STORIES OF AN LDS TREASURE HUNTER

WAYNE HAMBY

FOREWORD BY BRIAN W. HIGBEE, PMG, LLC

Plain Sight Publishing
An Imprint of Cedar Fort, Inc.
Springville, Utah

© 2016 Wayne Hamby

ISBN 13: 978-1-4621-1830-4

Published by Plain Sight Publishing, an imprint of Cedar Fort, Inc.
2373 W. 700 S., Springville, UT 84663
Distributed by Cedar Fort, Inc., www.cedarfort.com

LIBRARY OF CONGRESS CATALOGING-IN-PUBLICATION DATA

Names: Hamby, Wayne, 1944- author.
Title: Jaguars and cannibals : true stories of an LDS treasure hunter / Wayne
   Hamby.
Description: Springville, Utah : Plain Sight Publishing, An imprint of Cedar
   Fort, Inc., [2016] | c2016 | Includes bibliographical references and index.
Identifiers: LCCN 2015048103 (print) | LCCN 2016004502 (ebook) | ISBN
   9781462118304 (perfect bound : alk. paper) | ISBN 9781462126323 ()
Subjects: LCSH: Hamby, Wayne, 1944- | Mormons--Biography.
Classification: LCC BX8695.H325 A3 2016 (print) | LCC BX8695.H325 (ebook) |
   DDC 289.3092--dc23
LC record available at http://lccn.loc.gov/2015048103

Cover design by Krystal Wares
Cover design © 2016 by Cedar Fort, Inc.
Edited and typeset by Rebecca Bird

Printed in the United States of America

10 9 8 7 6 5 4 3 2 1

Printed on acid-free paper

For my sons, Matthew, David, Luis, and Joshua

CONTENTS

CONTENTS

FOREWORD

FLIGHT TO HAVASUPAI

You are about to embark on an unforgettable adventure as your mind and spirit carry you into jungles and distant cities full of sometimes tender and oftentimes dangerous encounters. There has never been a Latter-day Saint who can recount experiences quite like those that you are about to enjoy. Wayne Hamby was an LDS explorer, layman archeologist, US military veteran, orphan welfare organizer, gemstone miner, international marketer of those stones, world traveler, prison advocate who ministered to incarcerated convicts, and member of the Mormon church, all the while using up eight and a half of his nine lives along the way.

Death-defying experiences were a common occurrence for Wayne. You'll read about the time he had dinner with an Amazon tribe and found himself slated to be the main dish. His encounters with jaguars, snakes, poisonous spiders, and sea urchins are only slightly less spine tingling than his gun battles, street fights, and crash landings. After reading Wayne's original compilation of memoirs, I turned to him and simply asked, "Why are you still alive?" Despite all these adventures, readers will learn that Wayne also has a tender, compassionate, and spiritual nature. Several of his stories deal with his great love and care for those who are physically or environmentally challenged as well as his extensive work guarding the welfare of street children and orphans in South America.

Today, Wayne is courageously fighting his greatest battle and challenge in life. The latter stages of Parkinson's disease are now his highest mountain and deepest jungle. Whenever I meet him or call him to see how he is doing, he always tells me he is okay, and then he proceeds to tell me how blessed he is and what special thing happened that day.

Years ago, Wayne called to invite me to join him on a rare adventure to fly down to the beautiful Native American area of the Havasupai Reservation deep in the bottom of the Grand Canyon. Knowing this area to be rated as one of the most beautiful remote places in the world, I jumped at the chance. The Native Americans there, whose ancestors have inhabited the area for about eight hundred years, call themselves "the people of the blue-green waters." I had hiked this long trail from the remote southwestern rim of the Grand Canyon when I was a teenager living in Tucson.

When Wayne informed me that we were flying down with an ex-fighter pilot instructor named Dale Tingey and there would be horses brought all the way up to the top so we could ride them down, I was elated. Dale Tingey was the well-known, loved, and respected director of American Indian Services[1] until he retired recently at age ninety.

Arriving at the Provo Municipal Airport early in the morning, my good friend Trent Johansen and I met Wayne, another fellow, and Dale Tingey. His six-passenger, well-worn Cessna was packed with gifts of vegetable plants and small fruit trees intended for the Havasupai people. There were no roads into the Havasupai area, so after landing on a dirt road on the top of the canyon, a long horseback ride down the canyon walls to the Havasupai Village awaited us.

We packed into the "wing and a prayer" plane, and being 6'6" I drew the "lucky" seat of riding shotgun with this former fighter pilot instructor. This was a privilege I would soon regret. Wayne just chuckled because he had flown extensively with Dale and knew what was in store.

We taxied out and lined up for takeoff as Dale calmly asked everyone to cram forward into the front of the cockpit as best we could. He explained that at our altitude (which was approaching a mile above sea level) and with the amount of weight we were carrying, we would never get off the ground and clear the lake if we did not get as much weight forward as we could.

With Wayne and Trent hanging over the back of my seat, Dale gave the old engine full throttle. Roaring and bumping along, my eyes widened as we neared the end of the runway, which stopped just short of the Utah Lake shoreline. Bouncing and violently vibrating, we roared toward what I projected to be a lake baptism and possible drowning. Smiling and calm as that beautiful summer morning, Dale pulled back hard, and the old plane soared a full six inches above the runway and then skimmed just over the surface of the lake. We were airborne! The plane was no longer shaking, but the engine sounded like it was about to blow up with the strain. I looked out the side window, and we appeared to be at about the same elevation I'd expect to be at if I had been steering my ski boat along the lake's surface. The speed picked up, and we ever so slowly lifted, giving me a chance to breathe again and unlock my grip from the bottom of my seat.

I glanced at the relaxed pilot and then turned around to stare at Wayne, who gave a small smile and wink as if to say, "You haven't seen anything yet."

As we approached the Arizona border, I mentioned casually to Dale that my father, Major Bill Higbee, had flown P-51s in World War II, C-47s in the Berlin Airlift, an F-86 in Korea, and had spent several years as a hurricane hunter flying out of Hawaii. With that, Dale perked up in his seat and asked me if I knew how to fly. Already full of hot air, I assured him I could. With that, Dale pointed the nose toward Arizona and exclaimed, "See that peak? Head for it. I'm tired."

Curling down in his chair, he immediately pulled his hat over his eyes and went to sleep. Holding the controls with an iron grip, I was mortified. Slowly I turned my head around and looked into Wayne and Trent's faces. Trent's eyes were wide and full of fear because he knew all too well that I had never flown a moment in my life. Wayne was calm. I suppose he knew that he should already have been dead long ago and every day was a gift. I reassured them all that we were under control and that I would simply fly level and straight until Dale woke up. Just then, as we flew over some high mesas, *swoosh*, the nose of the old plane pointed straight up, and we were climbing like a fighter jet. The cabin echoed with the screams of grown men (I may have been the source of some of the high-pitched panic myself) as the little rickety plane, which previously could gain elevation only with great effort, was now rocketing up away from the ground.

I pressed the controls hard forward and nothing happened. With all men inside pressed back in their chairs, eyeballs bugging out and screaming away, Dale woke up, calmly glanced around to see what was taking place, gave a little chuckle, and somehow leveled the plane out. We had been caught in a severe updraft from heated air rising up the face of the mesas. Trent and Wayne thought that I had done this on purpose, and if they had not been buckled in, one of them likely would have choked me to death. I wiped the sweat from my face, turned, and let them know that of course it was not my fault.

After landing on the rim of the Grand Canyon (which was also exciting), we were picked up by a young Native American with a string of horses. We loaded the cargo onto the horses and enjoyed a beautiful ride down to Havasupai Village.

After wonderful experiences with these special people and swimming in the turquoise waters, we enjoyed our ride back up the canyon, passing hikers laboring up the trail from time to time. I felt guilty, but never for long. Once at the summit again, we packed the plane and bid our Native American friend good-bye. Dale fired up the old motor, and we roared down the dirt road, with the plane's engines straining and the rickety wheels bouncing. Just as we lifted off the ground, a car appeared around a bend in the road. I could clearly see the lady in the passenger's seat throw her arms up over her face in terror. Barely clearing the car, Dale wiggled the wings to wave good-bye to our friends returning on their horses.

We had crossed the wall of the canyon when, without warning, Dale abruptly pointed the nose of the plane straight down. To our shock and awe, we were flying straight down the sheer face of the Grand Canyon. Ledges and rocks quickly passed by. The floor of the canyon rose up to meet us. Once again, this relic of a plane was filled with flailing arms and the screams of grown men. With great vibrations from questionably sound wings, and with the entire fuselage shaking, we finally leveled off and began flying up the canyon valley, retrieving altitude. In a sweat, I glanced over at our gleeful pilot and back at Wayne Hamby who, after the initial shock, was laughing at us. Trent's eyes looked like his ancestor Vikings' might have looked when they were about to kill something— anything! It is embarrassing to confess that I think I left fingernail prints in the plane's steel dashboard.

Our flight home was thankfully uneventful except for the time we hit some turbulence. As I was looking out at the old wings flapping up and down, Dale told of how he recently landed at a prominent Native American chief's home on a remote dirt road and accidentally hooked the wing on a pole, which spun the plane out into the sagebrush and desert sand. When I asked how much it cost to repair the wing, he scoffed and patted the dashboard stating that he looked it over and the wing is just fine! I spent the rest of the flight waiting for bolts and screws to come flying off every time we hit bumpy air. I learned never to get into a plane with Wayne Hamby after that.

Over the years, Wayne stayed in touch. He mentioned once that he was writing his memoirs in a series of stories. I knew I had heard only a few of them myself and encouraged him to continue. His family encouraged and supported this effort as his health continued to fail.

When he eventually gave me a copy of his manuscript, I lay in bed one night to read his adventures, expecting to be mildly entertained. After my second story I sat up in bed and said to my wife, "These are truly amazing stories. I have never read anything like this," especially from an LDS author. Wayne is truly an LDS Indiana Jones! When Wayne asked for my help to see his stories published, my positive response was immediate. Prepare your mind for heart-warming stories of compassion and charity and to travel to far-off lands full of danger and adventure!

Brian W. Higbee
Professional Marketing Group, LLC

NOTES

1.   See americanindianservices.org.

ACKNOWLEDGMENTS

I am grateful to Brian W. Higbee, PMG LLC, who has championed this book from the early stages, encouraged completion of the manuscript, and also arranged for reviews and revisions by pre-editors and early readers.

A sincere thanks to Allison Wiser, Jordon Jones, Hillary Olsen, Kelsey Allan, Breanne Roper, Whitney Olsen McGruder, and Jennifer Woodward, who provided insightful editorial work as the manuscript was being developed.

I offer my heartfelt thanks to Lynnae Allred, Chelsea Jackson, Krystal Wares, and Rebecca Bird for the time, patience, and professional manner they displayed while representing Cedar Fort, Inc.

I am grateful for Dan Griffith, Stan Johnson, and Allan Pratt. These men have had a profound influence on me for good.

INTRODUCTION

I've had the opportunity during my lifetime to visit many interesting and exotic places. There have been peaceful and serene moments, times of spiritual manifestations, as well as times of extreme danger containing a certain degree of panic. There have been some amazing experiences. This book has afforded me the opportunity to relive some of those experiences, and in so doing, examine my motivations and the limits of my mortality.

Since childhood, I have felt a certain degree of confidence in my personal well-being, not because I thought I was better than anyone else, but because I really believed there was someone at my side who would take care of me. I have never said this to boast—I really feel humble and grateful for all the blessings I have ever been given. I have never flaunted this feeling, or consciously taken advantage of it. In fact, this is the first time I've talked about it, but it's always been there.

There have been various occasions during the course of my mortal probation where I have expressed optimism in recovering from a prognosis that had been pronounced as fatal by competent medical personnel. They were frequently offended, pointing out to me the folly of believing in things that were beyond the realm of realistic medical outcomes. Nevertheless, that feeling stayed with me over the years.

During the course of preparing the stories for this book, a most amazing and magical thing happened to me. There are some who will undoubtedly say they are "the imaginations of a dreamer," but be that as it may, when I sit down to examine these amazing adventures, the stories come alive to me. I can clearly see the things in my mind. I can hear them and smell them.

1

The largest leaf in the Amazon jungle is huge, six or seven feet in diameter. When you first see it you have to get closer to convince your senses it really exists. The veins of the leaf vary, but go up to two inches in diameter. It's lighter green on the bottom and a darker green on the top. As you run your hand across its surface it has a waxy, soft velvety touch. The first time I walked in the Amazon there was a fine mist falling and it was perfectly calm, quiet, and serene. I had taken one of the leaves from a palm branch and secured the whole branch on top of my head. It was amazingly efficient at keeping the mist, which had now turned to a light rain, from falling on my face, chest, and back.

For me, this was a true labor of love. There are times when people offer their condolences for my being tucked off in my room at the veterans' home where I live, but they don't understand I'm having the time of my life. Understanding where I've been is absolutely necessary to understand where I'm going.

SWALE IN THE PARK

In the early fifties, my family took a vacation to visit my grandparents in St. Louis, Missouri. We were from Heber City, Utah, a town of 2,100

Brothers Jim (left) age six and Wayne (right) age three.

people and the big city was frightening. I am sure we stood out like sore thumbs. My brother, Jim, and I had been advised by our mother to be extra careful not to talk to strangers, so we were especially watchful for any adults who might try and entice us to go off with them.

One of our first days in the city, just as our mother had warned us, a man pulled alongside in his car and tried to get Jim and me to go with him. We were both very frightened and ran as fast as we could go back to our grandparent's apartment. That experience marked us both deeply. During the rest of the trip we were very watchful and were constantly on guard against anyone approaching us.

Our grandparents, who were country people and had lived their lives in the small town of Ellington, Missouri, had moved to St. Louis for economic reasons. While there were many jobs to be had in the big city, Ellington had nothing to offer.

My grandparent's apartment was located directly across the street from a huge park. I don't recall the name of the park, but I remember that it appeared to be bigger than all of Heber City, Utah, put together. Jim and I went with our cousins over to the park and played most of the day. It was wonderful. There were swings, teeter-totters, sandboxes, and monkey bars. What more could a boy from small town Heber City want?

During the afternoon I somehow became separated from my brother and my cousins. Several times I thought I could hear their voices but each time I ran to see, it was never them. As time passed and the minutes turned into hours, I became increasingly alarmed. I passed by a brick building where old men were playing checkers, but after the experience with the man in the car I was too frightened to tell them I was lost.

I looked everywhere, but to no avail. Jim and my cousins were nowhere to be found. It was starting to get dark and I was on the verge of panic. I had walked the entire outer perimeter of the park following the fence because I knew my grandparent's house was on the other side of the fence close to the park, but I couldn't find it.

I wandered back in the direction of the building with the old men, but had decided not to go there. I was really torn about what to do. In Heber City it would have been easy. I could've spoken to anyone without the least degree of fear. As much as I wanted to approach them, I just couldn't. My mother's words rang through my mind time and again, "Don't talk to strangers!"

I had often heard my mother talk about the humility of the Mormon pioneers, and how they would always kneel in moments of need and pray as I had done with her many times. I was reassured when I thought of those times.

I walked in what I thought was a northerly direction until I felt secluded. There was a small depression in the ground, a little swale, with small trees growing around it. I reflected on what my mother had taught and shown us about prayer, and so I knelt down and began to pray for help. I was confident that God would hear me and answer my prayer, as He had done so for many of the pioneers that were lost, hurt, cold, and in difficult circumstances.

Although I was young and it was many years ago, I remember it perfectly. I stood up and knew absolutely the direction I should go. I turned slightly to my left and headed off in what I thought was a northwesterly direction. I walked directly to the gate in front of my grandparent's house and was greeted there by Jim and my cousins. They were unaware that I had been "lost," and I'm not sure that I told anyone about the experience at the time. For me, it was very personal, very profound, and very real.

I've always thought that my mother was a lot like the mothers of the stripling warriors, who believed their faithful mothers and were not slain in battle. My testimony of prayer has deep roots to my mother and to this incident in the park in St. Louis. Throughout my life I have been in dire straits many times and each time have had the reassurance of my testimony of prayer to guide me through.

JAGUAR

AMAZON

I believe that innocence, or maybe just ignorance, is often the best inocu-
lation for fear. Fear appears when you sense something unknown, something that threatens your well-being.

The problem is, most of these types of feelings often come to us sometime after the fact.

Sometime around 1983 or 1984, I started buying rough diamonds
from the Amazon basin, in the state of Mato Grosso, Brazil. I lived in
the Northeast state of Bahia, which required me to fly first to Brasília
and then to Cuiabá, in the west of Brazil. I then chartered a small plane,
which took me the last six hundred miles into the deep jungle.

I would normally fly on Thursdays or Fridays. This allowed me to
make my arrangements with the miners, who divided up their weekly
diamond production on Saturday morning, after which they were sold.
I would try to finish my buying as early as possible so that I could go
back to Cuiabá and wait for an evening flight to Rio de Janeiro. I would
arrive in Rio late Saturday night, get a good night's sleep, go to church
on Sunday, turn my diamonds into the transporter on Monday morning,
and then fly back home to Bahia.

The plane flew me deep into the jungle to a small village called Juína.
There was a simple dirt landing strip that stretched approximately three
miles outside of the village. As we approached the runway, the pilot would
fly his plane down very low, close to the ground, and buzz the village.
The remote village couldn't accommodate an air traffic controller, so this
basic and slightly more eventful method was the pilot's way of alerting
the locals that we were coming in for a landing. After announcing our

arrival, the pilot would circle around and then land on that bumpy old dirt runway that served as this jungle town's airstrip. The adventure didn't end once we landed and stepped off the plane; in fact, I would say that's where the adventure began. About twenty minutes after we arrived, a rickety old taxi would show up and take us to town.

Life in the little village took a little getting used to. The first time I visited Juína I remember asking the pilot what the red cloud suspended over the village was. He laughed and said, "That's not a cloud, genius. That's dust." He explained that the surface soil in that area was red clay and that during the dry months of the year, the sun beat down on the ground and heated it up, turning it into a red talcum powder. Cars drove by on the red dirt roads and the powder was thrown into the air, creating that red dusty cloud. It was everywhere. It was in the stores and in the houses. It was in your ears, nose, and just about every crevice imaginable. But the dust didn't last forever. After a few months it turned into a sticky, gooey mud. I couldn't imagine walking through six inches of that muck while wearing flip-flops or loose-fitting sneakers. The mud would suck them right off your foot. So, during the wet season everyone walked around barefoot. There really wasn't any other option.

The first time I was in the village, my arrival coincided with the arrival of a flatbed truck from the jungle. The truck was dragging a monstrous twenty-two foot anaconda secured by a rope tied just behind its head. That was the first time I had seen an anaconda so close. I was astonished at how big it was, not just in length, but also in diameter. As they pulled the huge snake around the city square, people were yelling and dancing. It was a giant celebration, and it was completely foreign to me. I asked the pilot why everyone was so excited. He turned to me and said, "Because the whole village is going to have a snake barbecue." My eyes doubled in size as I thought, "Oh, yummy . . . I think I will look for the salad bar first." But much to my surprise, it was actually pretty tasty. The strange reptile meat tasted very similar to the standard chicken breast I ate regularly back home. Sometimes, when you're in a foreign and inaccessible place, far away from the foods that you have grown up loving, it can be a real struggle. But in a way, eating that giant snake was comforting to me since I've always been the type of guy that, if fed well, could get along fine just about anywhere.

This next thing I want to tell you about is very difficult to write because it is so harsh. I just don't think its possible for me to help you understand the circumstances of the jungle without telling you the whole story. You see, in this particular area of the Amazon, there are hundreds of thousands of square miles that are overseen by a small group of only twenty or thirty policemen. Because the area is so large, it can take any-where from a few hours to a number of days for any one of the authorities to show up and enforce even the most basic laws. Such circumstances left the local people to regulate and enforce the laws. Sometimes the people would administer, what seemed to me, very harsh enforcement of the laws in order to provide some basic protection for themselves and their families.

Juína was an area that was known for producing diamonds, and was assumed by many to be a rich area, therefore making the small village a perfect target for criminals. I remember one time when two men from the south of Brazil came into this little village. They met a local taxi driver who drove a little Volkswagen Beetle. He stayed very busy, but was by no means considered wealthy. The men first killed him and then proceeded to steal his taxicab hoping to use it as their getaway car. They neglected to take into account not only that it was over six hundred miles to the nearest major town, but also that there was only one road in and one road out of the town. When the people in the village discovered what had happened, they quickly got on the radio and contacted the next police post, hoping to catch the two killers. After that it was a pretty easy catch. They simply blocked the bridge, making it impossible for the men to pass. When the men reached the bridge they were taken captive and brought back to Juína to be dealt with. When they arrived back in the village there was a bit of a debate to determine how to deal with the two thugs, but the dilemma didn't last long. The local people decided, in the best interest of themselves and their families, that justice could only be met by very harsh disciplinary action, which in this case meant execution by firing squad.

The two men were tightly bound and then taken to the central plaza of the village where they would be openly exposed to the community. Once the criminals were in position and the crowd had gathered, the decided punishment began. Every man in the village was required to share equal responsibility and participate in carrying out the sentence. If any one refused to participate they risked the persecution of the entire village. The men lined up in front of the prisoners and one by one, lifted their guns, aimed, and shot a single, potentially lethal, bullet. Once the firing squad had finished, the bodies were burned in place and left there for days. The charred remains served both as evidence of the crime committed and the justice served. The word of the execution spread fast. It was soon common knowledge that if you came to Juína to plunder or harm, you could expect to meet a similar fate as these two men. It was an amazingly effective lesson that served its purpose for a time. However, there were a couple other instances of crime shortly after my arrival. In one case, two miners were caught stealing from other miners. One was hanged and the other shot.

It was quite a shock to see this Old West justice, but with so few police over such a large area, it was a means to survival—the only way they could avoid being killed. In this rural mining area there were no buildings or safes. Money, diamonds, and other valuables were just kept in the shoeboxes in the miner's tents. The miners spent months or years risking their lives, hoping and praying that they would be able to make enough money to get them out of the dense and dangerous jungle and into a decent home somewhere in civilization. Considering the dangers and extreme toil they went through daily, it was a very serious thing to threaten the reward they had spent so long working for. For these miners, it wasn't simply the money that was important; it was the promise of being able to do something for their families. To provide something more than life inside a cardboard shack in the poverty-ridden slums in the south of Brazil. In the mid-eighties, when I first started going to this area to buy diamonds, the production was around five thousand carats per week. Over a period of only a couple of years, production soared to around fifty thousand carats per week. With a production explosion that extreme over such a small period of time, curiosity and the hope of fortune attracted quite the crowd. People came from all over looking for their "one big score," the one deal that would set them up for life. Combine this excitement with the particularly harsh frontier justice system of Juína, and you've got a pretty rough and desperate place. Do you remember the first Star Wars movie? Well, there is a scene where Luke and old Ben come up over a ridge. As they are coming over Ben describes Mos Eisley to Luke by telling him that he would "never find a more wretched hive of scum and villainy."[1] Well, that pretty much sums up my description of Juína.

8

A lot of very well-trained and professional diamond merchants from all over the world really put Juína on the map. One of these merchants, in particular, was a man from Israel. He set up a relatively large operation and built himself a home that was pretty typical of the area. To say that these homes were basic would be an understatement. They were made from simple 2 x 4s and some planking and were built on stilts about six and a half feet off the ground. The simple stilted homes may not have been very comfortable or strong, but they helped to keep everyone's belongings safe and dry during the seasons of torrential rains in Juína.

This Jewish merchant and I had become friends and had come to know a bit about each other's lives. At some point during our time together, I had mentioned my previous studies in ancient Hebrew, back when I was in college. Because of my somewhat basic, but nonetheless familiar understanding of Hebrew customs, he invited me to a very fine Passover meal he was preparing with foods he had brought in from Belgium and Israel. I felt quite honored to be invited to such a feast. When I arrived, my eyes bulged and my mouth watered; the food looked and smelled so wonderful.

Amidst the spread were almonds, a variety of sunflower seeds, and several other foreign nuts from the Middle East. I remember being astonished at the quality of food he had. He had also found and invited three other men from Israel to the dinner. We were called to the table where we gathered together and sat down, everyone anticipating the meal that awaited us. A few women placed trays of fabulous food in front of us. After a long procession of placement, one single space was left open for the final tray. It was a large tray piled high with stuffed cabbage; I believe it took two girls just to carry it. The instant they placed it on the table, there was a loud crack and, before we could comprehend what was happening, the whole floor went crashing down beneath us, and we dropped six feet to the ground, screaming. Apparently the beams that supported the floor couldn't handle any more weight. The tray of cabbage was the straw that broke the camel's back. Imagine sitting at a beautifully laden table one instant, and the next, plummeting through the floor! I'm sure my stomach tied itself into a few knots as we fell. It was quite a shock to say the least.

The aftermath was almost as extreme as the crash itself. The Passover was a very important event for this man, and for his guests, who had their whole lives wrapped up in the tradition of this meal. The impact of this experience was extreme. We tried to gather our wits, which had been scattered just as effectively as the wood floor and everything on the table. It took some time, but eventually everyone recovered and we got everything cleaned up. We ended the evening with dinner on the porch. Although the porch was not the most desirable location, it was still standing and that was more than could be said about the rest of the home. All in all, it wound up being a wonderful evening and quite the memorable experience.

I continued my buying for several years and then decided to venture off and do my own mining. I bought a piece of property that was nearly two thousand acres and about fifty-three miles from the village. My interest in mining peaked while I was doing some leisure reading at my home in the state of Bahia. There is a very good writer from South Africa named Wilbur Smith who wrote a book called *Men of Men*. It's all about the discovery of diamonds in South Africa. I learned that diamonds come up from inside the Earth in conduits that are similar to

Diamond mining operation in the Amazon.

volcanic structures called "pipes." In South Africa, years went by and the sun began to degrade the kimberlite. It faded in color and became very soft and chalklike. Much to the miners' astonishment, after lying around for years, this material suddenly became the mother lode of all diamonds. This was the material that had carried the newly made diamonds from deep in the earth up to the surface. It was the font of all diamonds. As the kimberlite was broken down, an unimaginable treasure trove presented itself.

I was out on one of my normal weekend buying trips when a property owner asked me if I was interested in buying his thousand-acre lot. He had a couple of small operations functioning on the property and told me he was getting diamonds from each of the places. I told him that if over the next two or three weeks he would dig out a couple of thirty-two feet wide holes down to bedrock, I would come back and take a look. He agreed and I went my way. On my return I was astonished to see how large of an area they had cleared the topsoil off of. They had two areas over sixty-five feet wide cleared down to bedrock. They had even chopped down two large trees and placed them over the top of the holes to be a walkway across the area. These makeshift bridges provided a perfect view of what was beneath. The topsoil, rocks, and debris were six to nine feet deep. The next layer was gravel, varying in depth anywhere from an inch to a foot. This was the most important level, the level that everyone paid attention to because it contained all the diamonds.

The shock of what I saw next nearly made me fall off the log bridge. In this area, the level below the gravel was a dark blue. When I had regained my composure I calmly asked the owner of the property, and several miners, what the blue material was. They said it was nothing, and it had no diamonds as far as they knew. The things I read in Wilbur Smith's book were flashing before my eyes. His description of what he found was like a textbook description of what I was seeing in front of me. Suffice it to say, the property was purchased and a mining operation was set up.

I built up my camp a mile or two down the river. A river divided my property from the indigenous people that lived deep in the jungle—the Cinta Larga. At first, they seemed docile and even childlike, but I soon learned that at the drop of a hat, they could turn into a wild and ferocious bunch of cannibals.

My lodging was simple; I had a small nylon tent held together by a framework of trees and a black plastic cover that hung over the top to shield me from the rain. I learned a lot of valuable lessons about how to prepare and cope with the rain. When the seasonal rains came, I had no way of knowing how powerful they could be. It was all foreign to me, a reminder that I was far from home. It didn't take me long to realize that a cloudburst in desert Utah is nothing compared to the torrential rain of the Amazon. For extra precaution and protection, I dug a one-meter deep trench around the tent, determining that would be more than enough depth to protect me during rainstorms.

The old saying, "Ignorance is bliss," is very true. I felt totally comfortable and at ease in the forest. There was no room for fear in my mind. Everything was beautiful, the trees, the birds, the big cats, the unrecognizable animals—it was all fascinating. There was one particularly beautiful bird that captured my attention. It was called a mutum. It was a large bird, at least as big as a turkey as far as I could tell, and was coal black except for a dark red comb on top of its head. I took many trips in my boat, almost daily, up the tributaries that went into the heart of the reservation. Thanks to a treaty I had negotiated with the Cinta Larga, I was probably one of the only white people to have ever ventured that deep into the interior[2] of that part of the unexplored Amazon. I had been told that many people from outside had been killed for trespassing on the land of the Cinta Larga.[3] If the Indians didn't get them, the exotic animals did. During my ventures there, I saw many allegedly extinct species, including the mutum. To witness these creatures was a once-in-a-lifetime opportunity and an experience not even commonplace for Brazilians.

This was such a fascinating place, and I was completely mesmerized. The sky was filled with birds, specifically the beautiful male and female macaws. The males were vibrant red, yellow, and blue, and females sported colors of blue and yellow. There were so many it was impossible to count them. The sky was filled with them

all day long. They were like the night stars of the day, decorating the sky with their beauty.

It was more than just the birds that fascinated me. To me, all of the big cats were equally alluring, but the most spectacular, the one that really captivated me, was the jaguar. There are a number of different ways a jaguar can be colored. There is the jaguar that most would recognize, with its familiar colors and patterns of spots, very similar to a leopard. There is also the breed with the spectacular jet-black coloration. There is a pattern to it as well, but it is so dark you can't normally see it. I have even heard tales of another version that is sleek and tan, much like the cougar from the United States. In the jungle, there are all sorts of dangerous and exotic animals wandering about, not just giant cats. I saw them close many times, usually just with a fleeting glance as they melted into the dense forest. They all raised the hair on the back of my neck, but the jaguar was in a class by itself. It was not uncommon to stumble upon the remains of a monkey or some kind of a bird that one of the cats had devoured as its latest meal. It was clear that they were excellent hunters and very strong, and that they had apparently been eating very well.

One night I was resting in the hammock outside my tent, reading by the dim light of a kerosene lantern. It was both wonderful and relaxing. When it was time for bed, I turned the light out and gently retired to my humble bed, a sleeping bag arranged on top of a foam rubber mattress. I zipped the tent closed and laid down to go to sleep. As relaxed and comfortable as I was, I was also prepared for trouble should it come. I had my reliable .30-30 rifle, and my 9mm semi-automatic pistol, both locked and loaded, ready for action. I didn't usually carry guns with me in the forest, but it was reassuring to know that should danger come lurking in the shadows of the night, I was prepared for it. I don't know how late it was or what caused my eyes to jolt open at that precise hour, but on this particular evening I woke up with all my senses tingling. Then I heard it.

"It" was a low-powered growl. I knew immediately, without a moment's hesitation, that it was the sound of a big cat. Although he was only growling then, I knew that the same source of that low growl carried a very powerful, low roar. Though difficult to explain, I felt the growl in my bones as much as, if not more than, I heard it in my ears. I had seen big cats many times during my stay in the jungle, but this was the first time I had felt threatened by one of them. The rumbling of the growl grew louder and louder, sending a stiff vibration through my entire body. All my senses were on high alert. I had maneuvered myself in a way that I was able to take the safety off of the weapons in case I needed to fire. I didn't know exactly how far away the threatening cat was, but I knew he was close, too close. I could hear his small movements, the intensity of his growling increasing dramatically. Something really had him riled up.

My thoughts raced and fell upon a memory. I had heard that the chief of the local village had recently been hunting and had shot a jaguar with an arrow but the cat darted into the dense bushes. It was assumed that the shot was not fatal and had left the cat wounded, and most likely thirsty for vengeance. The chief told me that he had had no choice; no matter how threatening, he had to go after the animal. If he left it wounded, he said, the jaguar would come back ready to attack. The chief was afraid that somebody from the village, perhaps one of the children, would come across the wounded animal in the jungle and lose his or her life. So, without hesitation, he pursued the cat. All he had for weapons were a couple more arrows and a knife.

He told me that he was frightened and didn't want to go, but his sense of fear was less than his sense of duty and responsibility for his people. He couldn't cowardly risk their safety for his own. He hadn't gone far into the brush before the big cat attacked. He was ferocious in his attack, but the chief was prepared and brought the arrow down in the animal's side right behind the shoulder. He had struck a fatal blow but the momentum of the animal had carried him forward with enough power to strike the chief before the jaguar died. The chief told the story with a good sense of humor, which reminded me of those old Boy Scout snipe hunting stories I grew up hearing as a kid. He lifted his shirt and pulled down his shorts on the side. There, glaring up at me, were big, deep scars on the side of his abdomen and the top of his leg. He laughed it off and chuckled as he told me he had been lucky that time. I let out a few exasperating chuckles; however, I think I found the story more terrifying than funny.

That story was replaying over and over again as I listened to the big cat growling outside my tent. My mind was flooding with all sorts of horrifying scenarios. What if this cat was wounded and vengeful? What if he was quicker to move than I was? I'm not sure how long the growling went on. It couldn't have been more than two or three minutes, but it felt like an eternity. It was as if every second of my life counted for a minute, and time was spinning away, endlessly. All of a sudden I could hear him moving again, and then, without warning, the growling stopped. I lay frozen in place, not knowing whether this silence was assuring my survival, or if it was the sound of my final moments. Time passed and my tense muscles slowly relaxed. With every minute that passed I became more assured that my enemy had left me in peace. I never did find out why he was so agitated or why he didn't attack, I just knew that I was greatly relieved that he didn't. It took me quite a while to get back to sleep. I awoke the next morning feeling less than rested, but with a new respect for the jungle and the big cats. Being so close to that powerful animal gave me an entirely new appreciation for nature, and especially for the jungle. I could no longer live in blissful ignorance. Knowledge of the jungle had brought me into a fascinating world full of wonder. But now, the fascination had a new companion: fear.

NOTES

1.   *Star Wars: Episode IV A New Hope.*

2.   The interior is any part of a country or location that is in the depths or far from the coast.

3.   The Cinta Larga's land consists of seven million acres, which are primarily unexplored.

ONE DARK NIGHT

BAHIA, BRAZIL

Under the best of conditions, the road from Teófilo Otoni, Minas Gerais, to Feira de Santana, Bahia, is challenging. It is nearly five hundred miles of a winding, narrow, and sometimes nearly impassable two-lane highway. It's a route you'll never fall asleep on. Unlike the American interstate system, Brazilian highways do not bypass the cities. Everyone basically drives as fast as their car will go, so strategic speed bumps called *quebra molas* (spring breakers) are placed every quarter mile or so within city limits to keep drivers in check. The same rule applies whether the town has five hundred or five hundred thousand residents. In fact, the smaller the town, the larger the speed bumps. Some of those bumps were large enough to have their own zip code, at three feet high and fifteen to twenty feet wide.

This is all just my way of saying that driving on Brazilian highways is quite an adventure, to say the least.

I had a morning flight scheduled from Salvador in two days. My plan had been to go to Feira de Santana, rest for the night, and then drive the sixty-two miles to the airport in Salvador the following morning. My flight was scheduled for somewhere around midmorning. Making the trip by car to Feira in less than nine hours would require dry weather, a road in good repair, and minimal traffic. I planned to leave midmorning, have lunch in Vitória da Conquista, and spend a restful night with my family in Feira.

There were two basic flaws in my plan. The first one was that it took longer to finish buying the emeralds I had initially gone there to purchase. The second was that I had received word that the stretch of road between

Vitória da Conquista and Feira de Santana was in terrible condition, and all but impassable. When buying gemstones in Teófilo Otoni, one should always gauge the time like shooting pheasants; you have to lead them or you'll miss. For me, it meant that I avoided planning flights on too tight a schedule, because I would either have to take the chance of going away empty-handed or miss my flight. Travel plans never run as smoothly as one would like.

Buying is always more difficult when there are big buyers in town. They like to sit in nice air-conditioned offices and sip little cups of coffee strong enough to take the rust off the bumper of a 1950 Nash. They pay higher prices because they don't like to go out to the mines or to the small cutting factories. Cutting shops are not air-conditioned and have very few creature comforts. However, if you want the best price, that's the place to go. I normally went to a small, hot, and sweaty stone-cutting office that belonged to a man I knew from Bahia named Lucas. He would provide

Diamond miners in the Amazon.

the security and make some of the initial selections of the goods I was interested in buying.

In many cases, it is cheaper buying in the cutting shops than buying in the mines because the illusion is gone. Miners often work for hours, days, weeks, or even months to find a good stone. When one is found, its value is equated to the toil, labor, and risk that went into its retrieval. It therefore instantly becomes the best stone ever found. By the time a miner closes up shop, catches a bus, and starts paying for a hotel and food in the city, the illusion is gone. Local dealers immediately point out all the reasons why the stone isn't worth much: the color, the clarity, the veil,[1] and about a hundred other reasons. They'll say, "You should just give me the stone and if I can get anything out of it, I'll cut you in."

At any rate, there were some buyers from Rio and the United States in town, and it took much longer than usual to make the buy. Putting together a lot[2] of emeralds is kind of like painting a masterpiece. No two lots will ever be the same, but could still be beautiful if done correctly. Quality and size have to be balanced with what the market will bear, what the current demand is, and what time of year it is. This time around, it was taking days for what could normally be done in one afternoon, but to leave before the job was done would have been a waste of the time and resources that it taken to get there in the first place.

I had most of the lot completed by the late afternoon, but I needed more time to finish it up. I desperately needed more of the smaller, commercial-size stones. I was promised there were more lots coming but they wouldn't be available until the next morning. I hated to wait, but decided it would be worth the trouble. I'd have a nice dinner and a good night's sleep, make the buy, and then drive to Feira in time to spend a nice evening before going to the airport. Well, 8:00 a.m. dragged out to 11:00 a.m., then noon . . . then 2:00 p.m. Nobody around there works from twelve to two. Everything shuts down, including the banks. Most of the time it's actually really nice, but not when you're in a hurry. I was wondering if those lots were ever going to arrive, and I was also wondering how much of my travel plans would have to be sacrificed in order to wait for the stones.

The stones finally came and for the most part, they were worth the wait. However, there were stones in some of the lots that didn't measure up, and the brokers had orders to only sell complete lots. I was intrigued by the lots, but I was also struggling to battle for the merchandise I wanted. I had packed my bags and paid the hotel during lunch. All I had to do was get in my car and go. The battle raged. Brokers ran back and forth to cutters and owners. Offers and counter offers. I told them to just have whoever owned the stones come and do it right now or I was gone. Nobody was impressed with my threats—they've all heard it before. They saw it as my way of controlling and positioning myself on the playing field.

Finally, the last lot was closed and paid for. I was finally able to leave and get started on the long drive. I thanked Lucas for letting me use his office as a temporary headquarters. He took my hand as we shook firmly, but before I took off, he gave me the stern counsel not to use the main road between Conquista and Feira. A local that he knew, Neginho (Little Black Man) had just come through there and told horror stories about the road conditions. Lucas suggested cutting off near Conquista and detouring over to the coast highway. I had never been on that road and was somewhat skeptical, but given Neginho's warnings, I decided it was my only real option.

The afternoon had been cool and cloudy. As I headed out of town it began to rain. It sure looked like it was going to be a long night. The 250 miles from Teófilo Otoni to Conquista was a gradual uphill climb, and the road was full of curves. You had to keep your eyes open for the cars and trucks coming down the hill because they sometimes crossed the centerline as they sailed down the hill on the turns. There was no railroad system in Brazil and consequently everything was delivered by truck. The highways were full of trucks, all overloaded and spewing thick black smoke. I could write a whole book on Brazilian exhaust pipes. They were in the middle of the truck, pointed outward. If you were sitting in your car with the window down, you would get a large dose of instant pollution. There were so many trucks that when it rained, the surface of the road had a slick, oily covering and instantly became very treacherous.

It was dark and raining by the time I got to Conquista. I stopped for a bite to eat and pushed forward. The crossover to the coast highway took a lot of time because it was a narrow, winding two-lane road full of large potholes. You couldn't let your guard down for a second.

There was a good stretch of road at one point, and I was just about to relax. Then WHAM! The pothole was so deep that the left front headlight broke coming up out of it. The rain had increased dramatically, the wipers on the car were terrible, and now I had only half the amount of light. I had to go very slow to avoid accidents. In Brazil, drivers aren't very good about dimming their lights, so combined with the other factors, the glare from oncoming cars made it nearly impossible to see. I had put in a cassette tape of general conference of the Church of Jesus Christ of Latter-day Saints and was feeling good in spite of the difficult road conditions. I slowed to be able to concentrate on the road and listened to the conference to keep myself in good spirits. It took a lot of effort to stay positive, considering the long drive, the weather conditions, and the worry of finding myself in another pothole.

I remember listening to F. Burton Howard's talk from the conference; it was one of the best I have ever heard. I felt the Spirit strongly, my heart was full, and I began shedding tears—lots of them. The witness of the Holy Ghost bore record to my soul not only of the truthfulness of the talk I was listening to, but also of God's love for me. Potholes, rain, frayed wipers, nor anything else mattered. I was no longer tied to earthly confines; I was soaring. Gratitude filled my heart with the absolute testimony that amidst all God's creations he knew who I was and he knew that I was driving in Brazil home to my family. He knew my name. He was speaking directly to me. My whole body was tingling.

I rounded a bend in the road and saw a police check station up ahead. I hadn't seen any cars for quite a while and assumed that no one would want to get out of their comfortable chair and bother with me. I was dead wrong. As I neared the check station, tears flowing freely, the guard quickly arose from his seat. As I neared, he flagged me to a stop. I pulled up just past him and tried wiping away the tears. I knew he would wonder why I was crying, but I didn't want have to explain the tears or my thoughts as I heard the talk. My feelings were very tender.

He was a huge black man and wore a dark uniform. In the darkness he almost disappeared. He asked for my registration and license. I knew the routine well. If they can find anything out of order, they will make things so miserable and difficult that the average motorist willingly pays to be able to escape. It seemed like a tragic end to such a beautiful experience. He asked if I knew that one headlight was broken and informed me that the stores in the village wouldn't be open for two days. He said that I would have to find somewhere to stay until I could get a new headlight and pay my fine.

"A fine? For *what*?" I asked, completely frustrated.

"It is illegal to drive with only one headlight," he said.

"Yeah, I know but it just happened; I'm a safe driver, but I can't help that the roads were left with gaping potholes everywhere," I complained, throwing my hands up in exasperation.

That was when I got the routine about "you foreigners think you can come down here and break our laws." Every word sounded like the cha-ching of a cash register. He had taken a very stern attitude with me.

I was puzzled as to why I could have just gone through such a profound spiritual experience and now be in a mess like this. Why had the Lord allowed this ornery cuss to cross my path? It seemed like blasphemy to be involved in a bribery negotiation after what I had just been through. How could I even think such things after what I had just experienced? The answer was I couldn't. So I didn't.

The guard's spiel continued on and he kept telling me how the local police don't earn enough money to feed their families, how bad the economy was, and how they could hardly afford to buy beer anymore. The more he told me about his financial woes, the more I told him about where I was from and how there are so many Santos dos Últimos Dias (Latter-day Saints) there. I told him I had studied the Book of Mormon for many years and how much it had changed my life. He asked to know more and I forged ahead. The more I explained, the more he asked. I'm not sure of the exact moment, but his whole demeanor changed for the better.

We spent a great deal of time talking and before I knew it, it was nearly daybreak. I needed to be going so I asked, "What do you want from me?"

The reply was soft and friendly. He wanted two things: he wanted me to drive carefully and he wanted me to send him a copy of the Book of Mormon. I told him I could do even better. I told him I'd send two young missionaries to bring him the book and answer any questions he had. He wanted to know if they could also talk to his wife. The burning sensation I had felt earlier began to return. My heart was now so full I thought it would burst.

I've reflected on the incident many times. Had he not felt the prompting to flag me down, we would have missed such an opportunity. I think back on that dark and rainy night with the broken light and the guard, and how the conversation went from hostile to redemptive. Had the Spirit not touched me so during a difficult and dangerous trip, I might have simply given him some money and gone my way. I would have passed by one of Heavenly Father's children who needed something better in his life. The Master had manipulated small details to allow that wonderful meeting to occur. Not only did I have a renewed witness of God's love for me, I also had a witness of God's love for that man.

I sometimes wonder how many other opportunities I may have missed over the years by not being spiritually in tune, or just being too preoccupied with my own little problems to be sensitive to those around me. There is tremendous power in continually asking ourselves if others can see in us the peace promised in this life for those who love God and keep his commandments.

NOTES

1.   While a veil in some gemstones is desirable, a veil in a diamond is bad, affecting the clarity and beauty of the stone.

2.   A "lot" is a group of gemstones being put together for a specific purpose, usually to sell.

SO THIS IS HEAVEN?

SALT LAKE CITY, UTAH

I didn't feel panic. I didn't feel pain. The fact is, I didn't feel anything. I didn't hear anything. The only one of my senses functioning was my sense of vision. I couldn't move my head, but I could move my eyes. All I saw was a beautiful, light colored, sky-blue heaven. I never imagined that heaven would be like this, just a sky blue, cloudless eternity. It was puzzling. I had always expected more than this from heaven, assuming I ever got there, which was debatable at this point in my life.

"So, this is heaven?" I'm not sure my utterance was audible, but soon after I said it, I heard an angelic voice.

"I'm here. I'll take care of you. Don't worry, you'll be okay." The voice was sweet, mellow, loving, and kind. My faith had been restored, my convictions vindicated. Angels really did exist! The voice was so peaceful, and so full of love. I felt as if I were being cradled in my mother's arms. I don't think I had ever felt so loved and cared for than I did at that moment. I wanted that angel to stay by my side forever. What a wonderful secure feeling. It must be something like a baby feels when its tummy is full, its diaper dry, and is warm and comfortable.

Wow! No wonder people raved about heaven being such a good place. I had just thought to myself about something I wanted, the angel staying with me, and instantly it was done. She stayed right by my side and continued to give me comfort and encouragement in soft mellow tones. Well, I now had two of my senses functioning, but couldn't feel a thing physically. I went somewhere for a while. I'm not sure where or for how long. When I returned, the angel, though still calm, was working feverishly to communicate with me.

"Stay with me! Stay with me! I'm here. Stay here. Stay with me!" She was pleading with me to stay, but I had no plans of going anywhere. I was really enjoying this experience.

It happened so fast that it startled me. Actually, it frightened me until I realized who it was. The angel had put her face directly over the top of my face with the top of her head pointing towards my feet. She was so close, and it happened so fast, it made me jump. I didn't really jump, just mentally. She didn't look like I had imagined an angel would look. Her hair color was a medium brown and very curly and frizzy on the bottom. And she had a few wrinkles on her face. I would have to ponder that one for a while. Do angels have wrinkles, or gray hair, or bad breath or whatever it might be?

"Can you hear me? Can you hear me?" She was very insistent and had urgency in her voice.

Whatever was going on had her very agitated. Gradually, over a period of a few minutes, I began to get my bearings. There were people yelling and even cursing and the sound of sirens. This was no heaven at all. I was still on Earth and my angel was a paramedic. Regardless, she was still an angel to me.

It was starting to come together for me. I asked the lady what had happened and she said that I had been injured in a motorcycle accident. To this day, I don't remember much about that because, as I soon learned, I had been unconscious before I even hit the ground.

Two weeks earlier, I had undergone major surgery on my large intestine. Their interior had been covered with diverticulitis, and my doctors had determined that a significant portion had to be removed. After a narrow escape with peritonitis in West Africa, I realized that this was no joke, and certainly not something I could put off. I had consulted with a surgeon in Salt Lake and had the operation in St. Mark's Hospital. My surgeon was excellent, and everyone at the hospital was very professional. It had been a very good experience, all things considered. The first couple of days weren't much fun, but after two weeks I had really made what I had felt to be a remarkable recovery and had been feeling very strong and confident.

At the time, I was living in La Paz, Bolivia, but for the surgery I had come up to Salt Lake City, where my family lived. Back then, my morning routine consisted of running three to five miles, at around 13,000 feet elevation in La Paz, and then doing five hundred sit-ups. That was followed by ten sets of ten pull-ups each. At forty years old, I was probably in the best physical condition of my life and it was that conditioning, no doubt, that had allowed me to get over the operation so well.

This particular morning had not only marked two weeks after my operation, but I really had been feeling remarkably well. It was early March, the weather had been nice, and I recall that it had been a beautiful day. I decided to take my motorcycle out for a spin around the valley. On a beautiful day like that, I would not normally have worn my helmet, but for some reason I decided to do so, because even though it was a nice day it was a little bit chilly. That turned out to be the best decision of that day. I was riding on the back roads between Pleasant Grove and American Fork, going around fifty-five or sixty miles an hour. I came to a spot in the road where the asphalt was cracked and a little bit loose and the rough surface began to jar the motorcycle and my body pretty violently. At that instant, the lights went out. The next part of that story, I woke up in heaven with a pale blue sky and my own personal angel.

The angel was still with me, helping me through what started out to be euphoria and ended up being pain and terror. As she and other emergency service people were checking me, it was obvious that I was paralyzed. I had no sensation whatsoever in my body. The contrast was really stark. One instant I was in heaven with my own personal angel, the next I was smitten with terror at the prospects of being permanently paralyzed.

The paramedics were being very slow and methodical, and taking great care not to move my body. With a spinal injury, caution is key. I was beginning to slowly realize the entirety of what had happened to me. I knew I had taken a bad fall and couldn't feel anything, and that terrified me. I had been relatively free of any major fears for most of my life, but I now felt a dread and fear like I had never felt before.

I've always been active. I've been running, climbing, swimming, jumping, or actively doing something with my body my whole life. My heart goes out to people who have been injured and lost the movement of their bodies. What a tragedy. To me, the prospect of not just becoming crippled, but becoming a paraplegic, was almost more than I could bear.

The one thing that hurt the most was thinking about running. I had always loved to run. Most people, it seems to me, run for health reasons.

I was one of those that loved to run. For me, there was escape, happiness, and pure joy in running.

Sometimes, when I was a boy, I would run home from the cemetery where I worked with my Grandpa Winterrose during the summer. Sometimes I would run in the foothills around a place known as the Red Ledges, near my home. It didn't really matter where. I just loved to run. Not being able to move, let alone run, struck fear in my heart.

The angel and her crew had been working to prepare me for the stretcher. The angel explained they had to be very careful because if there were any damage to my backbone, moving me the wrong way could be disastrous. How could it be worse than being paralyzed? There were a number of people on both sides of me now, in preparation for lifting me onto the gurney. On a given signal, they all lifted.

Years later, by bizarre coincidence, I met a spectator who had actually been at the scene, but had no idea that it was me being treated. They described the bloodcurdling scream of the man, (me, as it turns out), being lifted onto the gurney. That part I remember. I hadn't really realized it at the time, but the excruciating pain I felt was actually a very positive sign. It meant that I could feel something, and that was very good. At the time, however, I was in such absolute agony that I wasn't considering anything beyond the pain.

The paramedics were very efficient, and carefully but quickly took me to the hospital. My angel finally left me, but in the hands of a very competent emergency-room crew. I will always remember her kind, gentle, understanding nature. It came at one of the most difficult, trying moments of my life. Although I don't know her, I will always be grateful to her.

X-rays, CAT scans, and several other tests were performed to determine the extent of my injuries. It's kind of ridiculous, but as I think back on the experience one of the things that I was most upset about was that they took a pair of scissors and cut my Levis and an insulated Levi jacket off. It's really ridiculous to be concerned about something like that when there were so many more important things to consider, but I understand it's a pretty common feeling for accident victims. I waited for a long time, it seemed, before the results of the x-rays came back. Fortunately, there were no breaks anywhere, just a hairline fracture in one of the vertebrae.

Shortly thereafter, a supervisor from the hospital staff came in to confirm insurance information. As I've mentioned, I was living out of the country at the time, and had no health insurance whatsoever. Based on that and my inability to pay the bill, this man was there to tell me goodbye. He said they had done their part, to fulfill any legal or moral requirement, but the treatment was over. They weren't going to lose any more money on me. They told me that I could stay for a couple of hours while the shock I had taken to my spinal column was improving, but there would be no more medical treatment.

Over a couple of hours the feeling did come back to my body. What also came back was excruciating pain every time I made the slightest movement. I never thought I would be glad to feel pain, but once I understood what it represented as a sign of the state my body was in, it made me feel very grateful indeed. I inquired of one of the nurses, and she took pity on me and brought me some Tylenol. For the next couple of months, I lived with some very severe pains every time I tried to walk fast. Or get up from my chair. Or blink an eye.

This experience left me with a whole new perspective on pain. It raised my tolerance for pain and in a way that's a little hard to understand, and it also raised my appreciation for pain. Pain just means something, somewhere in the body is working. What felt like a long, ongoing experience of pain was actually a relatively short experience. I now appreciate being able to walk, even when it's with pain.

THE MUSIC MAN

FORTALEZA, BRAZIL

The man was relentless. Stroke after stroke he continued on. He was about two or three hundred yards out when I first spotted him. He had swum at least half a mile without even a break in rhythm. I hadn't heard of any Olympic swimmers in the area, but this man had no ordinary talent. Not only was he swimming a long distance, but he was swimming at world-class time. He obviously had a great deal of talent and was making good use of it. Every stroke was uniform and strong. He seemed tireless. I began thinking about how I walked and jogged for several miles along the beach every morning. I had conviction, but nothing like him. This was something different. I sat and watched. I had never seen such swimming ability in a person. When he disappeared from view and into the horizon, I arose and continued on. What was I doing with the talent I had been given? This thought troubled my mind all day as I encountered more people like the swimmer—two more to be exact.

Today was bartering day. I bartered for large quantities of beautiful, handmade linens and lace to supply our stores in Orlando, Florida, which my wife primarily ran.[1] It always amazed me how Brazilians produced a piece of Renaissance lace so cheaply. Brazil is one of the few places on Earth where the economic and skill levels make it practical to produce such a product. This rare lace is made in only two remote locations: the Madeira Islands and the interior of northern Brazil. It's not crocheted, but sewn meticulously with needle and thread. A piece the size of a card table takes over a month to make. It is the finest, most beautiful lace in the world. As I watched a woman weave the lace, I was amazed—just like when I had observed the Olympic swimmer. Her talent had been practiced and developed for years. Watching a lace-maker fabricate a piece of Renaissance lace is a marvel to behold. A visit to Fortaleza isn't complete without seeing a demonstration.

Fortaleza is a delightful city on the northern coast of Brazil with a highly developed infrastructure. There are high-class hotels, restaurants, and even an elaborate shopping center. However, the center for linens and lace was an old jail located north of the main commercial center. The cells have been transformed into little shops. I saw vendors hanging their fine fabrics from the corroded metal bars. There were also a number of vendors selling all manner of woodcarvings. I was struck by their craftsmanship. I was also taken aback with how little these people had; they had developed their talents, utilizing what resources were available to them. I felt insignificant as I walked through the halls of the old jail. I had been given so much yet had done so little.

As I observed the scene, I spotted bands of abandoned children attempting to sell linens and lace to all the visitors. There are approximately eight million abandoned children in Brazil. A number that high might seem completely preposterous, but it becomes more believable as you travel the country, especially in cities like Fortaleza, Rio de Janeiro, and São Paulo. The little children overwhelm you. Their roving bands wander from street to street, playing in or near open sewers. Numerous vultures are nearby, scavenging garbage in the streets, but this type of poverty causes a million heartbreaks, masking the many wonderful and delightful experiences to be had in Brazil. Poverty is everywhere, yet somehow the Brazilians are amazingly efficient and talented.

I don't want to paint too pessimistic a picture because I love the Brazilian people, but the reality of the problem can't be ignored. With so much poverty, there is a person around every corner looking for help—a coin, a half-finished sandwich, or even a smile. "Please, help me," is a phrase you hear often.

Being constantly surrounded by poverty tends to either soften or harden the heart. Unfortunately, many fall into the latter category. I've noticed that most Brazilians tend to ignore beggars. This makes them seem like they're hard-hearted, but they are just the opposite: they are warm, wonderful, outgoing people. They cannot aid the beggars because they are inundated with overwhelming challenges themselves. So where do they start? No matter where they start there is no end in sight. Who gets helped first? Does it make sense to help one when you can't help another?

It's the familiar story of the starfish. A storm had washed countless starfish onto the beach. A boy was going along, hurriedly throwing them back into the ocean. Soon, a man came along and asked the boy if he thought his efforts really mattered. With so many starfish on the beach, the boy couldn't possibly save all of them. His efforts didn't seem to make a difference. In response, the boy picked up a starfish and said, "It'll make a difference to this one," as he threw it back into the water. However, abandoned children aren't starfish—it's not that easy to throw them back. In most cases, there is no "back."

The parents are often still alive, but who knows where, and to give a few coins to one is encouraging ten more to ask. It's too easy to start a feeding frenzy. Hence, the warm, wonderful, outgoing Brazilians are forced to ignore.

In the Book of Mormon, a prophet by the name of King Benjamin spoke very clearly on this topic:

> And also, ye yourselves will succor those that stand in need of your succor; ye will administer of your substance unto him that standeth in need; and ye will not suffer that the beggar putteth up his petition to you in vain, and turn him out to perish.
>
> Perhaps thou shalt say: The man has brought upon himself his misery; therefore I will stay my hand, and will not give unto him of my food, nor impart unto him of my substance that he may not suffer, for his punishments are just—
>
> But I say unto you, O man, whosoever doeth this the same hath great cause to repent; and except he repenteth of that which he hath done he perisheth forever, and hath no interest in the kingdom of God.
>
> For behold, are we not all beggars? Do we not all depend upon the same Being, even God, for all the substance which we have, for both food and raiment, and for gold, and for silver, and for all the riches which we have of every kind? (Mosiah 4:16–19)

These thoughts crowd the mind as you walk down the streets of Brazil. The problem is so big it tends to overwhelm. We all need help, and we all need to give help. For those that would like to help, but can't because circumstances don't permit, King Benjamin offers this advice:

And again, I say unto the poor, ye who have not and yet have sufficient, that ye remain from day to day; I mean all you who deny the beggar, because ye have not; I would that ye say in your hearts that: I give not because I have not, but if I had I would give. (Mosiah 4:24)

God always provides a way out. We can't always see it, but it's there. We just have to look with spiritual eyes to see it. What I saw that day in Fortaleza with my spiritual eyes troubled my soul. I believe I had so many extraordinary experiences in South America because the people's needs were so great. I had been given so much but had done so little with what I had. It wasn't really guilt I was feeling, although that may have been part of it. It was something far beyond guilt. It was a call to action. And that was the day and the place the Lord had chosen to bring it to my attention. I was no stranger to third-world poverty. I wasn't seeing anything I hadn't seen many times before, but I was troubled all day. It kept gnawing away at me. I didn't want to be troubled in such an idyllic setting, but now the Lord had my attention. Now the real teaching could begin.

That evening, to calm my mind, I sat on the outside veranda of the Othon Hotel, enjoying some superb *picanha*.[2] As I ate, I looked out over the mosaic sidewalk and watched the myriad vendors as they set up their booths for the evening flea market. This was always one of my favorite markets. There were, of course, linens and laces, but also handicrafts and produce—fresh roasted cashews were always in great abundance. The meal and the evening were perfect. Satisfied, I rose to take my nightly stroll along the beach.

There were performers and artists of every kind on the beach. They each had a hat or a can placed on the ground near them for donations. They didn't usually get much—it all depended on how many tourists were in town. As I strolled, I noticed a particularly large crowd gathered about fifty yards ahead of me. As I neared the group, I began to hear the strains of what sounded like terribly played accordion music. I don't mean just a little off tempo, I mean really bad. It puzzled me how so many people were gathered around the source of this music. I thought it must be some kind of a comedic act. The closer I got, the worse it sounded.

If it was a comedic act, there was something wrong. I didn't see anyone laughing, or even smiling for that matter. What I saw were tears and looks of sympathy. Brazilians, as I have explained, are not touched easily. I don't recall having ever seen a group with such emotion on their faces. I pushed my way through the crowd to get a closer look. I couldn't believe my eyes. Seated in the middle of the circle was a man on a two-foot-square board. These boards had casters on each corner and were commonly used as transportation for people who were crippled or had lost their legs. These people wore gloves so they didn't scratch their hands as they pushed themselves along on the pavement.

The man playing the accordion had obviously been afflicted with some crippling disease that had left his body twisted and misshapen. Yet here he was, playing an accordion. He attempted to sing. It didn't really sound like much, but he was trying—no, not just trying, he was belting with determination. The people were casting money into his can from every direction. With such widespread poverty, it's common to see lots of hustlers, but this man wasn't one. He was a masterpiece. Hustlers fooled people, but these spectators weren't being fooled; their hearts were being touched. And so was mine.

The Lord is known to testify in threes. This was my third and most profound experience in Fortaleza. I had probably missed dozens of others. I knew I had been blind; there are none as blind as those who choose not to see. But thankfully, my vision was clearing rapidly. Many things became clear in that brief moment. Here was a man, sitting atop his board, stripped of all the expected physical attributes needed to ever consider playing an instrument. Yet he was choosing to put to use all he had left. He hadn't been given much, but for him it was enough.

This was my third wake-up call. I began to ponder. Not only are we put here to learn, but to experience, clearly understanding that we all have a purpose. Our callings may be manifold, but in the end, it all comes down to one thing: service, the surest cure I know. It can cure misery, depression, and frustration. It is God's incredible healing power. Here sat this crippled and twisted man, teaching us about service in action. That night he taught each one of us lessons that will be long remembered. As I listened, I felt the purity and beauty of the music touch my soul. It was from the heart of one of Heavenly Father's children. The scriptures teach us of various gifts given to God's children. On the surface, this man didn't seem to have many gifts, but in all reality, he was filled with them.

I will never forget the three individuals that the Lord placed in my path that day in Fortaleza. The determined Olympic swimmer and the talented lace worker both impacted me greatly. But it was the crippled man who changed my life. I will always remember him as one of my heroes and greatest teachers: the music man.

NOTES

1.   I first took a higher initial trip into the Northeast of Brazil to check the quality and viability of doing business with the people in the lace-making operations. We subsequently did some marketing and opened three outlets, two of them in malls and the other one in a tourist underline center. As I was doing a lot of stone business I would make visits and do business and give my wife some recuperation time for the busywork she was now doing with our three outlets.

2.   *Picanha,* pronounced pee-cahn-ya: the cap over the rump roast, considered a delicacy. *Picanha* is similar to tri-tip steak, but it comes from the opposite side of the muscle. The *picanha* is roasted in rock salt and left very rare. It is then sliced and lightly seared on a hot grill. Once you've eaten *picanha*, no other beef compares.

WILL ROGERS
JUÍNA, BRAZIL / AMAZON

Of all the times for the Cinta Larga to come, this was the worst. One or two peeked around the corner at first, and then fifteen or twenty seemed to appear from nowhere. It was one of those situations that look so bad that anything you could say would only make it worse. There were thousands of carats in the pile of diamonds on the table in front of me. The pile stood three to four inches high and looked like a fortune. It did have substantial value, but not as much as one might imagine. Almost all the stones were "makeables," which means they didn't have the standard octahedron shape of a diamond. To the untrained eye it looked like a bunch of pebbles. To those who knew, it was something quite different.

When I saw their guns and bows I knew I was in serious trouble. What would they do? Should I grab for a nearby pistol or try to talk my way through it? My scalp tingled. What I did in the next few seconds could very well determine whether I lived or died. I could feel every heart beat pulse through the veins in my lower throat.

The Cinta Larga were inherently suspicious. They came by on a daily basis to inspect our operation. They knew it was an American operation with American equipment that was purported to produce more than any of the monstrously inefficient systems produced in Brazil. But not understanding how it worked, they were suspicious in addition to the misgivings normally harbored by the natives for anyone from outside the reservation area (Area Indigina). These suspicions increased as they saw, yet knew nothing of, the strange equipment, which, to the locals, must have resembled something as foreign as a space rover.

Alluvial diamond mining operation.

The dredges roared as they purged the riverbed of its long-hidden treasure. I had two eight-inch Keene gold dredges with modified riffles that were designed to catch diamonds instead of gold. The concentrate separated by the sluice system was pumped into vibrating jigs to separate the diamonds. It was my own system, and I was very pleased with how well it was working. The heat was stifling, but it didn't really matter because all we wore were light cotton shorts. When the heat got to be too much, we just jumped into the river that separated the Indian land from ours and went for a swim. I can't remember being happier. The jungle was beautiful, the beautiful birds and wildlife were abundant, and the diamonds were beginning to flow. I didn't think life could get any better.

I had made a deal with the Cinta Larga tribe and agreed to give them a percentage of the diamonds I found in the river that divided our property. It seemed like a small favor to avoid getting killed. I knew they had killed over sixty miners less than a quarter mile downstream, so I didn't want to be anything but a good neighbor. There were always some of them present to monitor our production. I insisted on it. If there were ever a dispute, I would summon their people there to monitor. It was a good insurance policy. The problem was that they would grab their bows and arrows and take off at a moment's notice if any wild game appeared. They killed a gator very close to the dredge one day. A member of the local tribe casually walked up to it and drove a piece of rebar through its head. Though mortally wounded, the animal thrashed around and nearly grabbed his leg. It didn't thrash very long, though, before it was dead. That experience helped me appreciate their skills. They were proficient hunters and marksmen.

There had been a certain degree of jealousy and anger among the locals that a foreigner had come in and made a deal with the tribe to set up a diamond extraction operation. They decided after consuming substantial quantities of *cachaça*[1] that they would go in and mine on the Indian land as well. If some gringo could do it, why couldn't they? After all, they were Brazilians and this was Brazil. A group of about ten or fifteen of them set up a mining operation on the river that divided my property from the Indian reservation. When the tribe found out, they were furious. They went and really roughed up the miners and sent them away. One of the miners drank even more, and the more he drank, the braver he got. He went out by himself and started mining. When the tribe members found out, they dragged him back to their village in the jungle, killed him, and ate him.

A man from my camp went to the Cinta Larga village that afternoon and saw parts of the miner scattered around the central *maloca*, or tribal hut. He came directly from the tribal village to our encampment in absolute panic and said he was going somewhere where there were no Indians that came along with the diamonds. Several others joined him that day.

One of the older, more experienced miners said we should find out who the Indians' ringleader had been and hire him. I told him he must be crazy if he thought I wanted to be anywhere near that cannibal. He said I could basically have it one of two ways: either have the ringleader where I could see him or know where he was, or have him off hidden in the jungle imagining me as a pork chop. I did eventually hire him, but I kept an eye on him at all times. Even the big cats—the spotted jaguar, black jaguar and cougar—didn't worry me as much as that cannibal.

I recall one night having a big cat just a few meters away from my nylon tent roaring at the top of its lungs. The hair on the back of my neck stood on end, and I had my weapons locked and loaded. But even that experience didn't bother me nearly as much as the ringleader of the cannibals, a man I gave the name of Will Rogers. Think about it.

One day, ten or so Indians asked if they could catch a ride with my son David[2] and me to another part of their reservation. I agreed but felt some alarm when I saw them bring so many weapons. Whatever they were going to do had an ominous feel to it. Each one had many arrows, as well as rifles and pistols. We dropped them off and later found out they had killed over twenty miners who had started mining diamonds downstream on their property without permission. I felt sick to my stomach to think I had unwittingly taken them part of the way to do their dirty deed.

Eventually they came after me. The man who had sold me the property was twisted with a terrible case of greed and jealousy when we began to find diamonds. He told the Cinta Larga we had found a hundred-carat blue diamond and hadn't given them their percentage. I don't know how much you know about diamonds, but the most precious of all stones, the Hope Diamond, is blue. You couldn't even estimate the value of such a stone because there aren't any others to compare it to except the Hope. Needless to say, the natives weren't very happy with the gringo.

So there I sat at my table with thousands of carats of diamonds stacked up in front of me. And they weren't getting any of them. The stones weren't even mine, but I knew they would think I had gotten them from the river operation. They belonged to another mining co-op. I was inspecting and evaluating them to determine if I was interested in buying. I tried to explain, but the Indians didn't believe me. One minute they could be like little children and the next, transformed into ferocious killers. I felt ridiculous trying to tell them I was honoring our deal while sitting there with thousands of carats of diamonds they knew nothing about. It was obvious they were on the verge of losing control. I struggled to remain calm, but I had no illusions about their ability to exact any vengeance they deemed necessary. I had seen their work before and knew what they were capable of. Especially after learning that they had killed and eaten an errant miner near the edge of my property.

After the killing, a group of military police went to the reservation to confront them. The chief met them at the small sentinel outpost near the entrance. The soldiers were well armed and had acted quite belligerent toward the lone Indian. He didn't say a word; he just raised his arm and made a circular motion. Instantly, out of nowhere, fully dressed, armed, and painted warriors appeared. The military police were completely surrounded. One of the supposedly brave men passed out, and another shook in his boots. Needless to say, the warriors decked out in face paint and feathers presented a terrifying sight.

All these thoughts flooded into my mind as I tried to gauge what their intentions were. There was a lot of posturing, but as I learned from Ze Lope's[3] son, the bottom line was that part of them just wanted to kill me and get it over with—and, of course, take the diamonds. Another part wanted to kidnap me and take me to the village where I would be held for ransom. The thought of spending time near the grill they had used to cook the miner didn't strike me as a very good idea. It started to get ugly. Some were shouting and making threatening gestures. The old chief of all the villages, Lampiao, started slapping the side of my truck, which was parked outside the house. He was stocky and powerful. The blows sounded like cannon fire. I had stolen from them; I had to pay. The notion that I was innocent didn't seem to be of the slightest interest to them. They wanted blood—and they wanted it now.

I reasoned with them through the son, but his Portuguese wasn't very good so it was very difficult. But at least it gave me a chance. Most of them only had bows, so I knew I could take quite a few of them out with my gun. But I was far too outnumbered to even dream of coming out alive. And I didn't want to kill anyone. But if it came to fighting for my life, I determined I would make a good fight of it. Grandpa Winterrose used to use the expression, "Talking like a Dutch uncle." It meant you were a blabbermouth. And believe me, I was blabbing as fast as I could. There were some tense moments during which I prayed earnestly for deliverance. Precious minutes were going by. That was good. Time was on my side. The longer it took, the more time I had to calm them down. One thing was for sure: I didn't want to be anywhere near that village, especially at dinnertime.

Minutes stretched into seemingly endless alternating periods of threats followed by moments of relative calm. Because Brazilians take a long time to do anything, several very difficult hours ticked by like this. Finally, they began to have some doubts about the lies they had been told.

On a stroke of luck, the owner of the diamonds showed up to find out whether I wanted to buy his lot. This added to my credibility and made it plain to the Cinta Larga that he was the owner of the stones and that they had come from his mine. He had barged in unannounced. His eyes bounced back and forth like he was observing a ping-pong match. He was only too anxious to agree on a price and was practically running when he left. Nobody wanted to tangle with the warriors.

Finally, they agreed to go but said they would stay nearby until they decided what to do. Whew. Round one to the old gringo. But I had no illusions about being out of the woods, if you'll pardon the pun. I think part of the problem was they were hungry and wanted something to eat. I considered offering them some food, but, even though I'm no rocket scientist, I knew I didn't want them to associate me with their instinct of hunger. The phrase, "We'd like to have you for dinner," took on a whole new meaning.

Needless to say, I didn't sleep much that night. I wasn't quite sure what to expect. Turns out they had spent part of the night with the man who had told them the lie in the first place. He had them all riled up again. Only this time we were at my home in the jungle and they were more impatient than before. My reasoning didn't seem to faze them at all. The chief's son kept telling me that many of them wanted to kill me. I asked him if he felt the same way, and he said he was angry but unsure if he agreed with the others.

I had been praying fervently, both in my heart and on my knees. I felt prompted to ask about their history. The chief's son gave me a funny look and asked why I wanted to know something like that. I told him I had written a book about ancient America and the Book of Mormon, I had Cherokee blood, and I was interested. He pouted and said he had never heard of any such book. After some coaxing, he started telling me something of the history of his people. It was like being hit by a bolt of lightning. I knew instantly that I had found my way out. Although I had done extensive study, I had never supposed that the indigenous peoples in the Amazon basin were connected to the Book of Mormon. It had never crossed my mind, and I had never connected the two. And yet here was this man telling me the Book of Mormon story. I interrupted and told him the rest of the story. As I was telling him, he would translate to the rest of the warriors. The more I talked, the more he translated. The more he translated, the more flabbergasted the looks on their faces became. He said they were amazed because no one outside their tribe knew anything about their history. The floodgates were open. Light poured into my heart and then into theirs. They were absolutely amazed. They agreed to take me on a two-week trip into the jungle to the place of their origin. There were ancient ruins of some sort, and they told me that the leaders of the tribe go there once in their lifetime. I was intrigued, but for the time being I didn't want to go anywhere with them. I wanted to build the gospel foundation first—and I didn't want anyone to look at me as food storage when they got hungry.

Well, they were pacified and went home peacefully—and with a nice brown diamond in their bag. Just an extra little insurance policy. So now I can say that not only did the Book of Mormon save me spiritually, but it also saved me temporally. I find it very easy to bear witness of its truth. They told me this site in the jungle was the place where they emerged from the earth after having crossed a great sea. I told them of a tapestry that hangs in the anthropology museum in Mexico City that shows a migration of peoples from another land who came up through a hole in the ground that was somehow connected to an ocean. I also told them there were seven lineages in the Book of Mormon and the tapestry shows seven men coming out of a tunnel in the water. It then shows them going forward writing on the backs of turtles as they crossed the great waters.

It may not have lasted very long with the Cinta Larga, but I could feel the influence of the Spirit. It's that "peace . . . which passeth all understanding" (Philippians 4:7). I felt in my heart things would be okay. Relations were peaceable for a time, until this man, Mario, got them stirred up again and tried to ambush me and shoot me on several occasions. Well, we all get what we search for. Mario is now serving a twenty-two year sentence in a Brazilian penitentiary for murder and truck hijacking.

NOTES

1. *Cachaça* is an alcoholic beverage made from sugarcane.
2. My son David would often come to live with me for the summer months while he was out of school. He lived in Utah with his mother the rest of the year.
3. Ze Lope was the chief of the local village where my home in the jungle was located.

A TON OF MONEY

LA PAZ, BOLIVIA

When you hear the hyperbole, "a ton of money," it's usually used to signify large amounts of money, but it isn't really used to mean a literal *ton* of money. That's a ridiculous concept. Imagine you had a ton of money in the back of your pickup and were going down to the mall to buy whatever you wanted. How much do you think you could buy with a *ton* of money? To eliminate a lot of trips back and forth in your pickup, it might be best to have a good-sized backpack as well. And imagine the thieves. They'd be drooling all over themselves.

The notion of having so much cash conjures up some pretty powerful images, some humorous, some sobering. Let me tell you the story that I believe will give you a different take on this type of circumstance. In 1982, the price of precious metals, gold and silver especially, began to skyrocket and the demand was extremely high. I was in the gold refining business at this point and had people from all over the world bringing in gold they wanted refined.

We did some refining for a company that brought in raw material to Florida from Bolivia. In spite of Bolivia's reputation as a cocaine exporter, it is a country extremely rich in gold. The owner of one of the companies we were servicing made me a very lucrative proposal. He was a man who wanted to do big things in a big way. He wanted me to buy $150,000 in unrefined gold, and bring it back to the states for refining and sale. I told him that was a lot of money to start with, but he said, "If you're going to do it, you might as well do it right." I was reluctant, but he was anxious to start the ball rolling.

He gave me $150,000 in hundred dollar bills. I packed it tight into a Gillette shaving kit that I bought at Walgreens for seven or eight dollars. It was a small case maybe six inches by eight inches. I could buy a lot of gold at a good discount, but obviously I hadn't included anything for common sense. The closer it came to actually getting on the plane and flying to Bolivia, the nuttier this proposition looked to me. It was heady times in the gold market in those days and squeezed out any room I may have had for common sense and a lack of greed.

The flight to Bolivia was spectacular. I was flying with the airline Lloyds Aéro Boliviano. The pilot flew so close to the mountains that I wondered if he had flown a lot of small planes out of the jungle below. The Andes Mountains were beautiful with the dawn's red light reflecting off the snowcapped peaks.

We met our contacts, who whisked us through customs and on to a mansion in the residential part of town. This mansion was impressive, taking up one square block. I lay down and rested for an hour to avoid getting high altitude sickness. The airport had an elevation of 13,335 feet.

Over the next couple of days, we had numerous meetings with our contacts over the parameters of our operation. We had established that in order to get the percent profit we needed, we would have to go out to the jungle and buy for cash. Yeah, I know, it sounded crazy to me too. I met with a Chilean who had been doing this business for some time and was making a very good profit. I was still very reluctant, but over the next few days I decided to jump in with both feet.

We were now down to two things that had to be taken care of. One was security and the other was exchanging the money. Looking back at this situation now, it looks a lot different to me than it did at the time.

For the security, I hired a general from the Bolivian army who would take his Land Rover and provide whatever security we needed. Later on I found out just how swell this guy really was: he had once run over a man on the streets of La Paz, killing him and had then sued the man's family for damages to his car. When I asked him about it, he said, "Of course. What can you do when somebody gets in your way and damages your car?"

The last item was the exchange of money. In international business, arbitrage is a critically important factor and how well you do it may well determine whether you make money or lose money. The exchange rate was 240 pesos Bolivianos per dollar. Now that doesn't sound too bad when you first hear it, but when you understand the vast majority of the currency in circulation is five, ten, and twenty peso notes, you began to understand the complexity and absurdity of this deal.

When we started the exchange, we had numerous short and stout Indians walking up and down the vertical sidewalks of La Paz carrying large plastic garbage bags full of Bolivian currency. They used a strap that went around the plastic bag and was supported by their forehead. There were legions of little Indian guys all over the streets of La Paz. They kind of looked like a puzzle of *Where's Waldo?*

By the time all the money had been exchanged, I had over one ton of pesos Bolivianos. We transported all the money to the mansion where I was staying and stacked it on the shelves in the library. It was a large library and we had filled all of the shelves.

Yeah, yeah, I know, it still sounds crazy after all these years.

(Be sure and read the following chapters, "I Hate Your Guts" and "Popeye's Revenge," to find out how it turned out.)

I HATE YOUR GUTS

The trip from La Paz to the jungle through an area known as Las Yungas is one of the most incredible journeys of a lifetime. After leaving La Paz, you go over a mountain pass 18,000 feet in elevation. From there you travel along a narrow dirt road that is infamously the most dangerous road in the world. When it comes to passing another oncoming vehicle, there are times when one driver has to scrape against the mountain on the right side and the other truck has one of its dual wheels suspended in space. To make matters worse, most Indians don't have enough money to take the bus and frequently load up the back of large flatbed trucks. When one such vehicle slips off the road, it has several thousand feet before it reaches the bottom and everyone is killed.[1] There are no survivors. It's common to see accidents with seventy or eighty dead people from one miscalculation.

It's basically a two-day trip to get to the rivers where the gold is mined. The area I was interested in was at the confluence of the Mapiri and the Tipuani Rivers. We traveled the first day of the trip until it was late and everyone was hungry. We then stopped and checked into the local "hotel." Each room was small and had one side that was covered with chicken wire. There were no windows, and the showers were down at the end of the building. It was very basic living, but it was the best to be had in the area. This was not really a town. It was just a mining area and was located there because that was where the two rivers intersected.

Well, as I was very hungry, I went to the local barbecue restaurant, which was the only one there, and asked for some barbecued beef. The man nodded his head and went to work. I was busy talking to other people, but when I turned my head back to the barbecue, I saw one of the most disturbingly grotesque things I have ever seen. The "beef" was just the intestines instead of the meat. For those of you who like intestines, I beg your pardon, but for me it was just a horrible sight. What made it worse was the hunger I was feeling. I made such a fuss about the intestines that the man went in the back and came out with some bones and little pieces of meat that looked like they hadn't been fresh for quite some time.

I've always been a pretty good eater, especially when I'm hungry, but this was beyond my limits. At least he had moved the guts to the back of the grill. I was really hungry and I could plainly see the beef bones were very old and could have been sitting in a garbage can prior to my arrival. I don't normally think in these kinds of terms, but this was just one of those cases where the natural reaction was negative. I wasn't sure I had the courage to eat it but, since I hadn't eaten since the day before, hunger was overcoming my will.

When the food was brought to the table it looked worse than it did when I initially saw it. There were very small, meager strips of meat on the bones and the whole dish had a foul smell. Hunger does strange things to people, though. In this case it forced me to eat some food that I normally wouldn't have taken the time to throw in the garbage can.

The real message here, the thing to understand and to do something about, is that millions of people around the world eat food of this type, or worse, every day. Why? Because they're hungry, that's why. I've traveled extensively in Africa and South America, and have seen people eating food much worse than this. I have a picture of such a time burned into the back of my mind that I'm sure I will never forget: I was walking along a dirt street in western Africa and saw a young boy five or six years old cleaning dirt and rocks from a banana peel so he could eat it. And I don't want to forget . . . ever. The scriptures say that one of the gravest sins is that of ingratitude. When the media reports that Americans typically throw 45 percent of their food in the garbage, and then you become aware of the hunger of millions of people all across the world, it gives you a much different mind-set. I have a profound gratitude for food, not just to keep me alive but also to gladden my heart. I consider food one of God's greatest blessings.

What I wouldn't have given back then in the Bolivian rainforest for a medium rare rib eye. Oh, yummy. But instead, I went to my room and got my mosquito net ready for the evening.

I took a good shower and went to sleep on a clean bed. However, it wasn't without its challenges. I was awakened several times in the night feeling like a large insect had been crawling on my skin. Finally, I was so irritated I sat up and waited. I didn't have to wait long when a large mouse came up from behind the bed and jumped up and down the length of my body. I was so irritated by this time that I decided it was time for this miserable little rodent to pay the piper. I took out a small can of condensed milk and poured some on the floor. The mouse came again, but by the time I grabbed a shoe to smack him, he was gone. I poured a little more milk on the floor and left plenty on the top of the can. I held a shoe in the air without moving a muscle, and just stayed in that position until he appeared again. Well, that solved the mouse problem. The rest of the night passed in deep sleep.

NOTES

1. See http://www.bing.com/videos/search?q=Death+Road+Bolivia&&view=detail& mid=F3EA1AED2795E5DD64F9F3EA1AED2795E5DD64F9&FORM=VRDGAR.

POPEYE'S REVENGE

LA PAZ, BOLIVIA

he morning was a little chilly, which surprised me. I didn't know it got
that way in the jungle. I went outside to stretch and was panic-struck.
The general and my truck full of money were nowhere to be seen, and
not one of the gold buyers was in their rooms. I went to the manager's
office and was informed that the general had come back drunk and uri-
nated in her favorite flowerpot and she had thrown him out. This was
essentially the same story with all the gold buyers.

I was on the verge of total panic. One hundred and fifty thousand
dollars was a lot of money to lose in one fell swoop. At my frantic insis-
tence, the manager told me she thought they had all slept on the soccer
field. I went there immediately, and what a sight. The general was still
passed out on the open field, but the gold buyers were showing signs of
life. Because the general had been sleeping on the ground, he had big red
welts all over his body from chiggers. Chiggers are just little specks of
an insect, but their bites are much worse than any mosquito. The buyers
weren't in as bad a shape as the general since they had slept in the truck.
My day wasn't starting off too well either—I was beginning to feel sick
and achy.

Back at the hotel, the owner wouldn't let the men back in until they
apologized and paid her the daily rent. We finally got everybody in functioning shape and sent out to the mining camps to buy the gold. I felt very
uneasy about letting them go anywhere with even a portion of the money,
but I was already committed and thought it best just to play it out. Besides
the money, there was something troubling me deeply. I was feeling awful
by this point. Not just the kind of awful you experience when you have

a cold or upset stomach. This awful felt different. I hated to admit it, but I realized it was probably the so-called food that I had eaten the night before that was causing the problem.

Pushing through the sickness, I selected two members from the group and we headed for La Paz in the general's truck with the other half of the money. I figured if I were going to lose it, it would be better to only lose half and then finish the buy the following week. It was a long and arduous full-day trip to La Paz, and I was getting sicker by the minute. Within an hour or two out of the small town, I was mostly unconscious, with only brief moments of lucidity. At one point, I awoke and found myself in what appeared to be a small hospital, with a nurse inserting IV needles in both my wrists. I had had IVs put in before, and normally there is very little pain associated with the process. This time, though, was much different. It was excruciating. Over the next day or two, I continued to fade in and out of consciousness, but even through my delirium I could feel the pain of the needles in my wrists.

When I finally did wake up, it didn't take long for me to decide that oblivion was a better state to be in. I had a fever, headache, body aches, and a stomach that was rumbling like Mt. Vesuvius. The most alarming thing by far, though, was that both IVs had apparently perforated the blood vessels and gone out the other side, directly into the flesh of my forearms. I looked like Popeye. Imagine each of your forearms the size of a one-liter bottle. I called the nurse over and began to complain about the state I was in. She was very crabby and said something about gringos always complaining. Her bad temperament turned into instant animosity when I asked her why she hadn't checked the IVs during the night. Because of the commotion, a doctor soon arrived. He removed the IVs and told the nurse to put new ones in. I told the doctor I didn't want this nurse doing anything else to me and to give me another more competent one.

To say she was irritated is putting it mildly. And unfortunately for her, the remaining task happened to be a distasteful one. The physician ordered her to empty the bedpan. She looked like she had been attacked by a reincarnated bat from the witch street in La Paz. With a pitiful look on her face, she marched forward, arms extended, gagging at every step. She entered a utility room and although I didn't see her anymore, I heard the bedpan as it hit walls and tables, ending up on the floor.

Miraculously, the initial gold buy was completed without me, and had even produced a good return. After being discharged from the hospital, I rented the home of the newly elected president of Bolivia, Hernán Siles Zuazo, and lived there for nearly a year buying and selling gold. I had many more adventures, too many to recount here. At the time, though, I felt this home offered me a degree of safety from the outside world, insulation from those same adventures into which I seemed to continually find myself. It did have a large, twelve-foot tall concrete wall that surrounded the entire property, but I thought the real protection the home offered was due to its status and the notoriety because of its owner. Surely a home of this category would be recognized for the power it would surely command. Eventually, I discovered I was completely wrong, and the home was just another set of new clothes for the emperor. In Bolivia, no place is as safe as you want to believe it is. I found out President Zuazo had lived in the house during a previous presidential mandate and all of the president's associates had been machine-gunned within the walls of the home. While this fact was disconcerting, it wasn't until the wall around the palace was machined-gunned as well that I decided it was time to say goodbye.

HURTIN' URCHIN

ACAPULCO, MEXICO

The force of the water was so powerful I was nearly helpless before it. The next wave rolled toward me, and I could feel myself being drawn toward the rock.

I marveled at the unseen danger I hadn't perceived from the beach when I had decided to swim to the large rock in the middle of Acapulco Bay. I hadn't really paid any attention to the waves near the rock. From that distance and at that angle, the sea had looked calm. The gently rolling waves had seemed harmless.

I kicked my legs and swam as hard as I could, but this turned out to be one of those good news/bad news deals. I found something solid to help propel forward, unfortunately it was a sea urchin. Just as I was kicking my leg, trying to get some force to carry me forward and away from the rock, I jammed the arch of my foot down on the sea urchin.

There is no way I can adequately describe the excruciating pain of having my arch suddenly jammed full of sea urchin needles. Each one of the needles was approximately the size of the lead from a standard pencil and very much the same color. I wasn't quite sure what had happened, but a friend who was swimming nearby, also unaware of the intensity of the waves, swam over and verified my fears. "Oh, wow, looks like you stepped on a sea urchin."

It was one of those times you just want to call a time-out, or king's x, or anything else you can think of. "Just stop the pain, just stop the pain," I kept repeating to myself.

We are very much creatures of our own particular frame of reference. That is, we are shaped and formed, to a great extent, by the things we encounter in our everyday affairs, whether they are good or bad. Or, more specifically, by our reaction to the things we encounter. I recall once, when I was about five years old, I lost my balance and fell off the kitchen counter top. I came crashing backwards and hit the floor hard. Naturally as a little boy, I began to cry. I cried for a minute and, realizing there was no one else at home to hear me, I stopped. What's the use of crying, if no one can hear you? I drew on that lesson during this experience. I stopped complaining, and got down to the task at hand . . . getting myself safely back to shore.

I knew that getting back to shore was only the first of my problems. I tried not to focus on how I would remove the spines from the bottom of my foot. I just shut everything out and focused on one thing, lengthening my strokes so that I could get back as quickly as possible. Stan Johnson, a tremendous swimmer and great friend, helped me get all the way back to shore.

There must have been some kind of toxin in the spines, because the pain was more than I'm sure it would have been if I had just stepped on a nail or piece of glass. The other factor in the pain equation was the salt water. Salt water on an open wound is what's known as a "big owie."

When I got to shore, I obviously couldn't stand because of the spines in the arch of my foot. My friends helped drag me out of the water, making quite a fuss of it. Just as they had moved me far enough out of the water to examine my foot, an older Indian man walked by. He had very pronounced Indian features and dark skin. The only clothing he wore was a pair of athletic shorts and a belt with a knife.

He walked up, looked down at my foot, and with a smirk said, "You gringos are all the same. You just never seem to learn."

Even though I was fully occupied with my present situation, I felt annoyed with this man and his caustic nature.

"You want me to pop them out for you. It wouldn't be the first time. I have had lots of practice with all you gringos that come here and get in trouble."

I asked him how he intended to pop them out, and he said with the point of his knife.

"Yeah, right! And what do I do while you're popping these spines out of my foot with your knife?"

He exhaled, rolled his eyes and said, "You just lay there and try to act like you're a man, although it's all right to yell a little bit, because it hurts like the devil."

I didn't know what else to do, so I nodded my head in acceptance. His knife was long and in the shape of a bowie knife, but the blade wasn't quite as heavy. He had me roll over on my stomach and lift my foot in the air. Holding the knife near the point, he very studiously and calmly began to pop the spines out of my foot. He was right about one thing. It really did hurt. The pain had moved to a new level now. It was so intense that there was a kind of numbness that had set in. He continued on, popping and pulling them out one after another. My revulsion turned to respect as he methodically and rapidly removed the spines.

Finally, the task was complete. He had removed all the spines from the arch of my foot. He had me try to put some weight on my foot to see if there were any more spines broken off under the skin. There is a nerve cord in the arch of the foot much like one of the nerve cords connected to the teeth. I obviously had a spine broken off under the skin because whenever I put any weight on my foot, it was just like a dentist touching a nerve with one of his little pointy tools. The pain was excruciating. He had me lay down again and he tried to find and remove the broken spine, which was broken off about a quarter inch under the skin. Every time he tried to remove it and the point of the knife touched it, I felt intense pain. Ironically, one of my traveling companions was a dentist. He arose, and went quickly to the hotel. He returned with a small pair of tweezers, a bottle of rubbing alcohol, a razor blade, and a cigarette lighter.

It must have been easy to read my mind, because before I could protest, the Indian said, "I think that's the only way that it can be done."

The dentist, without uttering a word, took out a Gillette razor from its package, broke it in half and held it over the flame of the cigarette lighter. When he felt it was sterilized, he poured rubbing alcohol on the bottom of my foot. I hadn't thought that the pain could be any more severe, but I was wrong. This was the most painful thing yet. The Indian, now in the role of mentor, told me to hold still, and it would soon be over. The dentist cut down on both sides of the spine, but inadvertently touched the spine several times. Each time he touched it, no matter how lightly, it sent shock waves of pain through my body. Finally, he had the flesh opened up enough to put the tip of the tweezers in the incision. He quickly pulled the tip of the spine out. What an incredible relief. Each phase of the experience had taken me to a new level of pain awareness, and I was glad it was over. Before I had a chance to even sigh, though, the Indian told me I needed to immediately go back into the salt water off the bay.

I told him he was crazy if he thought I was going back in the water. It had hurt enough the first time with the spines still in my foot. I had no desire to feel it again, this time with my foot resembling ground beef. He told me that he knew from experience, if I didn't immediately get back in the water and let the salt kill the bacteria and sterilize the wounds, I would develop a serious infection that could cost me my foot or even my life. He said he had seen it happen many times before, and there was nothing better than salt water for cleaning an open wound.

In the end, I took his counsel and hopped back into the water, paddling around for fifteen or twenty minutes to let the salt clean the wound. I got out of the water and had my foot disinfected and wrapped before I went back to the hotel to rest. I was fearful of putting any weight on my foot the next day, but when I did it felt astonishingly good. My foot was sore for a few days, but not as bad as I had expected, and it healed quickly. I developed a soft spot in my heart for the Indian and his expertise in treating my foot.

I can reflect on different situations in my life that have been very dangerous, but didn't look so on the surface. As miserable as each situation was, there was something to be learned from the power of unseen waves.

TINY FINGERS

FEIRA DE SANTANA, BAHIA, BRAZIL

A midst all the people we see and meet in the places we go, there is occasionally one person that obviously has a bigger impact on us than all
the others. Allan Pratt is one of those people, and not just for me, but
for many other people as well.

Back in the mid-nineteen fifties, I would occasionally visit one of my
friends in Kemmerer, Wyoming. Every now and then he would babysit
his neighbor when the parents went out of town. Whenever their trips
coincided with one of my visits, I would help him babysit. My friend
and I were about twelve years old and the neighbor boy was several years
younger than us, but over the space of numerous visits and years, he grew
older and we all became friends. His name was Allan. But as the years
passed by, I stopped visiting Wyoming and we lost track of each other.

Many years later, after having lived in both Bolivia and Brazil for
several years, through a series of circumstances I wound up moving to
Kissimmee, Florida. My first Sunday there, I walked into church and
much to my surprise Allan was the bishop there. Although I didn't recognize Allan at first, I recognized his parents, who were also in the ward.
His father was a delightful man, always smiling. His was the kind of face
that you don't soon forget.

I went to see Bishop Pratt soon thereafter, and told him where I
had been and some of the crazy things I had been doing over the years.
I wanted to start new and get things right with the Lord. I was afraid
that Allan, now Bishop Pratt, would think I was a hopeless case, but he
didn't. He gave me something very precious: trust. Allan had the ability
to see things that other people couldn't see—to look through common

prejudices and see what a person was really like inside. His taking the time to trust and reassure me was a major turning point in my life.

We rekindled our friendship, and over the course of many chats, he asked a lot of questions about Brazil, about which he was quite curious. We wound up spending a lot of time talking specifically about the profound problem of abandoned children there. He was a physician by trade, and he focused on that issue a great deal, eventually rounding up some of his doctor friends and putting together a foundation to help these children.

One day, we were discussing the situation of the abandoned children in Brazil, and I told him that it was estimated there were over eight million abandoned children living on the streets in Brazil.

He wanted to know if there was something more he could do to help these children. Allan and I put together an exploratory trip, with the dual purpose of buying some more emeralds and deepening our understanding of the abandoned children situation.

Seeing a particular situation on television or reading about it in a magazine can provide some background, but there is nothing like actually being there to give you a feel for what's really going on. When you walk

The sweet little orphan children.

the streets of a Brazilian city and are approached by hundreds and hundreds of people, both young and old, asking for help, it really gets to you.

These children weren't only abandoned on the street. They were also murdered on the street—regularly. It was such a common thing for death squads to murder children that Rede Globo set up a camera crew on the second floor of a commercial building in the central part of Rio de Janeiro to film it happening.

In one video, there was a group of homeless children sleeping on cardboard in front of some stores. Men dressed in black just walked up and started shooting. The ones that weren't killed immediately were shot in the back while trying to run away. These were children from ages five to fifteen. If it's so common that a news crew can film it, you know there's a lot of it going on. It is tragic and it is wrong, whatever society says about it.

There was a time in the 1980s when death squads were hired by merchants to keep these abandoned children away from their stores, so as not to bother their customers. These death squads had originally started out, ostensibly, with the purpose of killing criminals that had paid off the police or someone in the judicial system, so that they could do their crimes and not have to spend time in a penitentiary for it. From there, it progressed to merchants having people killed if they didn't pay their bills, or if somebody offended them in some way, or, in the case of these abandoned children, if they were bothering someone's customers. It was just amazing that day after day the television station would show the death squad's daily count on the midday news shows. They usually totaled from two hundred to three hundred murders per day.

It was in these circumstances that Allan and I made our visit to the Assemblia de Dios orphanage in Feira de Santana, Bahia. Bahia is a state in the northern part of the country. Having lived in that city, I was well acquainted with the children there. On this particular trip, I had set up an appointment with the director for that afternoon. Allan and I stopped at the central shopping district in town to buy food and supplies for the children. While at the store, Allan had what turned out to be a tremendous idea, which was to get two enormous bags of Peanut M&Ms for them.

The director warmly greeted us upon our arrival. He and his wife were amazed at the food we had brought for the children. At first, the children were a little bit withdrawn, but soon warmed up. They were careful not to be pushy or to offend, but they wanted to be close. They wanted to touch and be touched. It seemed to be an innate yearning in their starved souls. Their tiny fingers held tight to my hands, arms, legs, belt loops, and every available finger. They were not demanding or aggressive in any way. They just wanted to be loved. A simple touch would suffice.

Love is an innate human desire. I recall hearing about an orphanage in Romania where the infant mortality rate was sky high. Eighty to ninety percent of infants were dying. They did a study and compared it with several other facilities and discovered in most other orphanages the babies were held and talked to. In this particular orphanage, though, they were fed but given no love or attention. They simply died—not from any sickness, but from lack of physical contact and expressions of love. One day they were alive; the next, they were dead.

The director gathered the children into an open-air pavilion made of concrete that was about two feet high with a fifteen-foot-long corrugated metal roof to keep the rain away. In all, there were 113 children living in the orphanage aged from newborn to eighteen years old. Allan started handing out the M&Ms and their eyes lit up. This was a special treat for the children because they didn't get sweets very often. They came up to us one by one and took their share of the candy. Some of the kids had gone to the bathroom and were not there when the candy was handed out. The older kids had said they'd hold on to so-and-so's candy for him or her. My first reaction was that of skepticism, but that was soon replaced by admiration. They didn't take one piece of the younger kids' candy. They held it and gave it to the others upon their return. The director and his wife had done an amazing job of nurturing these children in a family atmosphere of honesty, integrity, and selflessness.

After the candy had all been handed out, the director asked if there was anything they could do for me. I smiled and told him that he and the children had already done far more for us than we had done for them. He turned to the children and asked if they would like to sing for us. They eagerly agreed.

I took a seat in one corner of the bowery. Having sung together often, each child knew his or her place—the little ones in front and the bigger ones in back. They sang a hymn and it was wonderful. I thought my heart was going to jump out of my chest as the music penetrated my soul. I started to move, assuming they were finished, but they had only just begun. They sang another song, even more beautiful than the first. And then another and another. I sat there listening, totally absorbed in the spirit of the singing. There were tiny fingers wrapped around my hands. My heart was so full that I thought it would burst.

In some way, far beyond my ability to explain, the Lord touched my spiritual eyes and opened my understanding to something about each of those precious little children. As I made eye contact with each of them, I understood something about who they were, what they were like before they came to earth, and what the future would hold for them. Love. Pure love seemed to course through me. Each one of them was a spirit child of our Father in Heaven. I knew them. I had known them before. They were familiar. They were family. God knew each one of them and He knew their names. It was the first time in my life I fully understood how precious each of us is to our Father in Heaven. He understood, knew, and loved each and every one of them. Not just collectively as a group, but individually.

The songs continued as I moved my gaze from face to face. They seemed to be waiting for their turn. Each child wanted not just to be loved, but also to love back. It was the same with each of them whether they were teenagers or toddlers. Every time I made eye contact, it was as if they had been expecting me. I've had some humbling spiritual experiences, but never like that one, before or since. Some faces were small and brown. Some were black and had braided hair. Some had cute freckles, but they all had one thing in common. They were children who had been sent here to gain experience. They each had a mission. Some would become teachers or nurses. Some would become wonderful fathers and mothers with little ones of their own to care for. They would make a difference in the lives of others. Tiny fingers wrapped around my hand. They were already fulfilling a portion of their mission; they all had a capacity for love which "passeth all understanding" (Philippians 4:7).

When all was said and done, they had sung for over an hour. The cords of our hearts were stretched to the breaking point. It was hard to hold back the tears. All these little random faces we'd see in the big cities now had a personality and a name. They each told us their own name and in unison thanked us for the candy. Allan's choice of treats had really been inspired. I've visited many orphanages all over Brazil, but I found more love at this particular place than anywhere else.

Although 113 seems like a relatively large number, it was a tiny fraction of all the displaced children in Brazil. And now that we were personally in the orphanage with the children, they were far from being random statistics. They were warm, wonderful, giving, and loving little children, soaking up all the love they could find.

The truth of the matter was that they were much more fortunate in the orphanage than children left to fend for themselves on the streets of Rio de Janeiro or São Paulo. Here at this facility, they could expect food, a place to sleep, and a chance to learn something. What they wanted most of all was to be loved.

TADEU

FEIRA DE SANTANA, BAHIA, BRAZIL

I feel a deep sense of frustration with the whole abandoned children situation that exists in Brazil. There was an even deeper frustration with the plight of the handicapped children. They looked like castoffs that nobody wanted to bother with—or so I thought. There was a couple from Utah that was in Brazil to adopt children. They had connected with us through our charitable foundation in Florida. I took them to an orphanage located in the center of town, and I was delighted to see that they really took an interest in a particular little two-year-old boy. His name was Tadeu.

Tadeu didn't pay attention to anything or anyone. He just sat there on the concrete floor and rocked back and forth, soaked in a pile of his urine. The only thing he had on was a washable diaper. Everything surrounding him went on with what appeared to be perfect regularity. There were about a hundred other children in the facility, but he was by far the most severely afflicted, and nobody paid any attention to him.

At the orphanage, there was a wonderful, saintly woman who often came to volunteer her time helping the children, as I learned from the workers there. I saw her pass by all the other children and go directly to Tadeu. She started talking to him as you would any little baby. She was showing him love. It was as if someone had turned on a switch in his face at the sound of her voice. He obviously recognized it. He was giggling and laughing. What a joyous sight! The Utah couple was very interested in what was going on with this little spirit, and they wanted to know if there was something they could do to help him. The caregiver discussed some of Tadeu's needs as she cleaned, bathed, and played with him. She said there was an item that was expensive for them that might be affordable for the American couple.

What she suggested was a little walker so he could push himself around. She said it could provide an entirely new life for him. The couple readily agreed. We immediately went to buy one for him. At the current exchange rates, the walker was very cheap. We put it in the car and went directly back to the orphanage. We took it inside and got it set up. While doing so, this amazing lady talked to and caressed Tadeu. Beyond all possibility, he seemed to understand everything she was saying to him.

Soon it came time to try the walker out. When the lady brought him over and put him in, he became so excited, squealing with joy! His little legs were kicking frantically. In a short period of time, after some teaching and patience, he was pushing himself all around the office. There wasn't a soul in the room that didn't have tears streaming down their cheeks.

As wonderful and important as the walker was, it wasn't the thing that was needed the most in that orphanage at the time. The thing that was most valuable was the love of that volunteer lady for this little castaway. It was the love and generosity of this American couple who bought the walker without hesitation. As Paul said in the New Testament, "Charity never faileth" (1 Corinthians 13: 8).

THE BEST DAY

FLIGHT BETWEEN SALVADOR, BAHIA, AND SAO PAULO, BRAZIL

The passage through the tunnel of bamboo trees on the way into the Salvador airport was always an enjoyable one for me. It seemed safe as I passed through it. From there on, the arrival and check-in procedures had their normal monotonous routine. First, pay the driver. Without fail, he always had that glint of hope in the corner of his eye that there would be a little something extra for him as he placed my bags on the cart, as if it were the single most important thing he had ever done.

Next was the ever-present wait to check my bag and get a boarding pass. Since they didn't assign seats, there was always keen competition to get a favorite spot. Not that it really mattered. The smoking seats were on the right side of the plane and the non-smoking on the left. This, of course, meant that no matter where you sat on the plane you were going to have to breathe someone's cigarette smoke. Everything had a maddening sameness. It was all so predictable.

It was a typical travel day. Just like hundreds of others I had made over the many years I had spent living and traveling in South America as a diamond dealer. The trick to safely traveling with large quantities of diamonds or money was to detach oneself from the trip—to insulate oneself from people, places, and things. I couldn't afford the luxury of talking to anyone and risk being outed as a dealer. It didn't matter that I wasn't carrying any gemstones on me on this particular trip. Old habits die hard and I couldn't let my guard down. The stakes were high—with how much money I usually had on me, it was my life and livelihood that were on the line.

The flight was almost empty and afforded the luxury of being able to have some space, which meant privacy. No one was near me, which offered safety. Rule number one: don't talk to anyone; don't trust anyone. After having gone through hundreds of airports all over the world, anonymity and detachment had become second nature—out of necessity—despite how hard the adjustment had been for me. There was always a sigh of relief when a plane lifted off. It meant some degree of safety. There is safety in distance in my line of work.

While I sat, I reflected back on a trip that I had taken once, passing through Rio de Janeiro. It had appeared easy on the surface, but had turned out to be very difficult.

I had been buying large quantities of diamonds in the Amazon basin and emeralds in the city of Teófilo Otoni. The life of a gemstone trader was a rough existence. It was a cutthroat world, one in which you didn't want to be the man who showed up for a knife fight, only to find out it was a gunfight. At that particular time, there was a man who wanted my diamond mining property, who knew I was travelling and making purchases, and in an attempt to sabotage my business, had alerted the authorities that I would be coming through. When passing customs in Rio, the inspector punched my name into the computer and it lit up like a Christmas tree. I just caught it out of the corner of my eye. I could tell they were talking about me, and that meant trouble. I had a large lot of expensive emeralds with me and, all of a sudden, I had a terrible sinking feeling in the pit of my stomach. The inspector closed his station and asked me to come with him into a back room. I knew from experience there would be a strip search, all my bags would be searched, and my electronic goods would be confiscated. I knew the routine but, for the most part, had been able to dodge the bullet up to this point.

The negotiations were intense but rapid. It was a time when Brazilian residents, of which I was one, could buy a certain amount of tourist dollars to travel with. The difference in exchange rates at that time was very advantageous. You could, in essence, buy dollars at a discount. And that was what the inspector really wanted. If I would let him buy my quota of dollars, I was not only off the hook, but I had a permanent escort through customs anytime I wanted it. I wasn't planning to use my tourist dollars quota anyhow, so I was more than happy to oblige. However, people in positions of authority have a tendency to be greedy, so I had a hard time believing that was all he really wanted. But unsearched, I acquiesced. I can't tell you the relief I felt once the plane was finally airborne.

Back on my present trip, though, I was irritated and grumpy that on a nearly empty plane a teenage girl and her brother had sat next to me. The last thing I wanted was a couple of bratty kids to compromise my detachment, and distract me from my nice, anonymous, electronic chess game. I was sitting on the aisle and had to stand up to let them in. She sat next to the window and Dennis the Menace sat next to me. Within a couple of minutes, I had to get up again and let the boy out. He went to the next row and sat directly behind his sister. Almost immediately he began tormenting her and continued to so throughout most of the trip. He pushed the seat forward, kicked it, yelled, and made a terrible nuisance of himself. I was really irritated and did everything to avoid making eye contact or having anything to do with either of them.

The flight from Salvador to Brasilia took about an hour and a half. It seemed like a day and a half. I wasn't sure how long the second leg from Brasilia to São Paulo would take, but whatever it was, I knew it would be too long. The stewardess asked everybody to remain in their seats because we had a number of passengers boarding. I really wanted to get another seat but felt prompted to stay.

The new Brasilia passengers began boarding. Quite a few had gotten off, so there was now even more space than before. I thought I would wait to see how many got on and then reconsider moving. Among those entering, there was a missionary from my church wearing her name tag. The plane was nearly empty and there were many spaces available. The sister walked directly to my aisle, though, and motioned for me to move so she could sit in the empty seat next to me. I stood and let her enter. Because of her name tag, I had the advantage of knowing who she was. There was the whole plane full of empty seats and she chose to sit next to me.

Actually, as I was to find out, she probably intended to sit next to the teenage girl more than she planned to sit next to me, but the Lord knows how to do things. She introduced herself to the girl and her brother. At first I didn't say anything. Probably out of guilt. Since I had been so crabby and detached, I was ashamed to admit that I was a member of the Church. The sister was friendly, but seemed to be preoccupied about something. She had a strained look on her face.

I reached into my bag and took out my Book of Mormon, which I showed to the missionary. She looked at the book and then at me, with a look of utter astonishment on her face. Then she began to sob uncontrollably. I was completely at a loss of what to do or say. I tried to calm her, but the tears kept coming. Her dilemma had caught the attention of those around us. Everyone seemed to be looking at me as if to say, "What did you do to her?" I shrugged and felt an intense desire to crawl under the seat. It was quite a while before she regained her composure to be able to talk. She was returning home to her family earlier than scheduled. Though she spared me the details, she believed her newly divorced family would disown her for returning early.

For some reason, it was critically important to her to return with another Church member. She didn't know what to expect when she arrived at the airport, whether there would be family or not waiting for her. She had prayed fervently for another member to be on the trip with her, but there had been no other missionaries scheduled to go home at that time. She was desperate. When she realized she was sitting next to a member, it was just too much for her to handle. The tears were of joy and gratitude. Her heart was full, but mine was breaking. The Lord had blessed this sweet sister by providing her with me—but I did not feel worthy to be a blessing to anyone. I had deliberately avoiding making personal contact with those around me.

The girl next to the window ask the sister what the matter was and the sister began a conversation in which we both explained to the girl and her brother the basic tenets of the gospel of Jesus Christ. The girl and her brother were also experiencing family problems. As I recall, the parents were separated and the children were living with another family member. The Spirit was palpable by the end of the trip, and the sister missionary, the girl, and I were all in tears as a result. We had each borne our testimonies, touching one another's hearts. Here had been an excellent opportunity to share the gospel with people who needed and wanted it. My old habit of shutting others out had nearly robbed me of that opportunity. And if I ever had any doubt about miracles, they were dispelled that day. Dennis the Menace had stopped his tormenting and had become involved in the conversation. Both he and his sister wanted the missionaries to visit them. The sister took their names and address and promised to have the missionaries contact them. I have no doubt that she did.

We arrived in São Paulo, and now the sister had to face her moment of truth. Would her family be there to greet her? She was apprehensive. We walked together, and thankfully there were some of her family members there, although her father was not. I know she was disappointed, but buoyed up by her spiritual experience on the plane. My heart was breaking for her, but I'm sure her testimony and spiritual sensitivity saw her through. She was satisfied that the Lord hears the prayers of His righteous servants.

I walked out to the curb and hailed a taxi. I left the airport and asked the driver if he could take me to Villa Carioca in Ipiranga, wait for me to leave my bags at my brother-in-law Ramon's house and then take me to the LDS temple. Naturally, mention of the temple and the Santos dos Últimos Dias brought a discussion that ranged over a broad spectrum of gospel topics. He was like a dry sponge. He wanted to know everything and he wanted to know it right then. There were questions he had asked ministers on various occasions and had never received answers to. I was able to answer his questions and it was evident that he knew the answers he was getting were true. The Spirit in that taxi was incredibly strong and it filled my heart. I felt like I could fly. The Spirit was burning in me like it never had before in my life.

All I had done was put myself in a position to allow the Lord to use me to help others. By the time we got to the temple, we were both in tears. I got his name and address to give to the missionaries. He told me he knew where there was an LDS chapel and promised to go the following Sunday. We parted as brothers.

I walked into the temple with my spirit soaring. The peace and confirmation I felt are beyond my power to describe. While in the temple, a young man walked up to me and called me by name. I nearly fell over. At first I didn't recognize him. Then it all came flooding back to me.

Several years earlier I had taken ill on a flight to Brasilia. My son David, who was twelve at the time, had been with me. We had to get off the plane and go to a hotel so I could rest. I couldn't go any further. I didn't know what was wrong, but I felt terrible. The next day I forced myself out of bed and went to a hospital. The doctor took one look at me and said, "You've got hepatitis." I wanted to know how he could diagnose me without even touching me. He told me to go look in the mirror. I was shocked. Both my skin and my eyes were a very pronounced yellow.

The doctor told me there was nothing he could do for me, but he did suggest a fruit called *lima*. According to him, some people had found relief from its juice. I went back to the hotel. David was about ten or eleven at the time and was frightened. He didn't know if I was going to live or die. Actually, I wasn't too sure about that myself. By happy coincidence, which was certainly Heavenly Father acting through his servants, we met the missionaries near the hotel and they were a tremendous help. They gave me a priesthood blessing, brought me some *limas*, but most important of all, they gave some much-needed support to David. Not only was he worried, but he wasn't accustomed to the food and hadn't been eating very well. The missionaries took him to a McDonalds and David really went crazy over it. He brought back sacks full of hamburgers to have later.

Well, the voice I heard calling me in the temple was one of the elders who had taken care of me. What a day. I wasn't sure my heart could take any more. What a blessing to have met him there. He lived in northern Brazil and was there on a temple trip. It was no accident that he happened to be there at the same time I was. The Lord was really telling me something. I was convinced that life couldn't get any better than that. It was like years of experiences and blessings had been packed into one day— instant condensed spiritual experiences. I had no idea what I had done to deserve such a day, but I was really enjoying it.

I caught a taxi near the temple, but within a mile, the driver said he didn't know the area I was going to and I would have to take another taxi. It took a while, but another taxi finally stopped. This driver knew the area I was going to, but he was a nasty, crude, foul-mouthed character. I was a bit disappointed since the day had been so incredible up to that point. I didn't want anything to spoil it. I hated to see it end on such an unspiritual note. This guy wanted to do nothing but complain. He asked what I had been doing in the area and I explained I had been in the temple.

"Mormon, huh?" Yeah, he had heard about it. There was a chapel close to where he lived. According to him, all churches were the same. They only wanted your money and didn't give anything in return. He vowed they would never get anything from him.

As we drove, he asked questions. I answered and he asked more and more questions. I had a powerful witness that I should bear my testimony with him. By the time I was through, we were both in tears. What an outpouring of the Spirit. By the time we got to Ipiranga, he was pleading for the last of three Portuguese Books of Mormon I had been carrying with me. The first two, of course, had been given to the girl on the plane and the first taxi driver. When we arrived at Ramon's house I retrieved the book from my suitcase. The taxi driver was as eager as a child at Christmas. He was on fire and asked if he could be baptized that night. I told him what he needed to do to accomplish that. He said he was going to church on Sunday and promised to read the Book of Mormon. He gave me a big hug and departed.

I was in shock. I have never had a day like that before or since. There have been some wonderful spiritual moments, but never a day so packed full of them. I hope someday I fully understand all the Lord's purposes beyond the obvious. Until that happens, I can say that besides the Lord giving me my family, that was the best day of my life. I have often said that when you're angry, upset, or frustrated, the surest cure is to do something good for somebody else. In the end it all comes down to service. Charity. I hope to never hide my light under a bushel again (Matthew 5:15). The Lord truly knows where to place his people so they can help one another.

SPIDERMAN

HONG KONG

As I looked up, I noticed every eye was looking at me. My Afghan friend Nasim was seated at the same table, but didn't seem to be attracting much attention. We were in a small Chinese restaurant far from Hong Kong's busy tourist area. Westerners were evidently not a common sight in that particular neighborhood. It struck me as kind of ironic that they were interested in me when in reality, it was I who was interested in them. Spending my early years in Heber City, Utah, was a wonderful experience. Even though I've wandered far and wide, I still consider it my hometown. But even as a child I was conscious of the fact that everyone looked like me. Everybody spoke the same language and almost everyone was a member of the LDS Church. However, I've always had a curiosity about other peoples, countries, and cultures.

Initially, Aunt Geneva was my source to the outside world. She traveled extensively around the world and always brought me stamps and coins from far away, exotic places. I still have my stamp albums. Each time I would get a stamp from a new country, I would look up everything I could find about it. What language they spoke, what commodities it produced, what it exported, how big it was, and how many people lived there. I was always fascinated with the information. I was hungry to know more. I vowed to go to these places when I got older and I've had the good fortune to do just that in many instances.

So doing business in Hong Kong really wasn't an accident. I've had a lifelong yearning to go to such places. And now at last, here I was. The normal tourist areas were great, but I wanted more. I was curious to see how the people really lived. And clearly from the attention I was getting, this was no tourist area.

A dim sum restaurant is quite an experience. Little Chinese ladies wheel big carts around the restaurant with collections of different bite-size options in little baskets. Many of the dishes were a real mystery to me. I had no idea what I was eating. When I found one that was particularly good, I'd ask for another of that type. I hoped no one would tell me what I was eating. If it tasted good, that was all I wanted to know. When you're finished, you call one of the ladies over and they count how many dishes you have. That's how they charge. A set price per plate.

We left the restaurant and went to the movies. It was in English, but it had Chinese subtitles. Again, we were far from the tourist areas and, as far as I knew, the only Westerners in the theater. It was a large building and the seats were set at a steep angle. We were about ten minutes into the movie when a group of men behind us started smoking. That was a mistake.

Afghanis are warm, wonderful, respectful people, but you don't want to rile them. Nasim was offended that someone would be smoking and especially blowing the smoke on us. He turned around and really ripped into them. They responded back angrily. It instantly became a very intense situation. Nasim was yelling at them in English and Pashto. They were hollering in some Chinese dialect. Nobody knew what the other one was saying, but everyone understood the opposing parties weren't happy. There was a lull in the discord and it appeared to be over. Some others in the theater were also voicing their displeasure and the men put out their cigarettes.

Everything seemed to be okay, but I was still on guard for any possible problems. Still wary, I caught some movement out of the corner of my eye. I had the impression that one of the men was throwing something, but we weren't splashed with soda or hit by popcorn, so I forgot about it. It seemed like nothing. A few minutes later, I felt an insect on my neck. I brushed it away and kept my focus on the movie. Minutes later, I began to have a terrible itch on the palms of my hands. From there it moved to the soles of my feet and to my crotch. Which brought up an interesting dilemma of how to solve that problem in public.

The palms of my hands and the soles of my feet were on fire. I had never had such an itch in all my life. It really felt like my hands were burning. I was extremely uncomfortable, but determined to shrug it off and concentrate on the movie, but I couldn't. I had to strain to hear, so I stuck a finger in my ear and discovered that it was swollen nearly shut. I told Nasim we had to go. Outside he used the neon light from the city's signs to check me over and the look on his face told the story. I was shocked to see huge, pronounced, dark red welts on my arms. Nasim said my face was very puffy. Breathing was a labor. We grabbed a taxi and headed for the hotel.

I remember the shock I felt when I entered the hotel and saw myself in a mirror. There was an enormous round, red welt on the side of my neck where I had brushed away the insect. There were red welts everywhere. I think it was at that moment when I realized the man behind me in the theater had thrown a spider on me. I asked to see the hotel doctor immediately and was told it would take an hour or so to get him there. By this point in time, my eyes were nearly swollen shut and breathing had turned into a terrible labor. Nasim demanded we catch a taxi and go to a hospital.

The driver didn't speak much English, but one look at me told him what we wanted. He roared away into the hills of Hong Kong. It took about ten minutes to get to the hospital. The driver dropped us off and left. Nasim helped me inside. I couldn't walk on my own. My ears were now completely swollen shut, my eyes narrow slits, and I was fighting to breathe. There was a language barrier, but when all was said and done we found ourselves at a convalescent hospital on a dark and lonely hill with not even one doctor on staff. A man explained that they only took care of old people, not sick people. I sounded pretty ridiculous, but all I wanted was another taxi and to get to a real hospital.

It took about fifteen minutes for another taxi. By this time I was in and out of consciousness. I realized I was dying and there didn't seem to be anything I or anyone else could do about it. The taxi arrived and Nasim was very aggressive in getting him to take us to the hospital in a hurry. You have no idea of what a Hong Kong taxi driver can do if properly motivated. Bless the Afghani. Nasim supplied the motivation. He had taken the he-dies-you-die approach. I actually think I had a better chance of surviving the spider bite than I did the wild ride.

Shaken and gasping for breath, my throat nearly swollen shut, we finally arrived at a hospital that could treat me. Nasim and the driver carried me into a waiting room that looked like it was the size of a football field packed with people. The man behind the desk handed Nasim some papers and told him to fill them out. Nasim tried to explain my dilemma, but the man said everyone was important and they had all arrived before me. They had problems too. Nasim wadded up the papers, threw them in the man's face, reached over and grabbed him by the shirt and gave him the "If he dies, you die," routine. The body language crossed a lot of linguistic lines.

I had always had a feeling of invincibility. I can't explain why, but it's always been there. This was the first time I had to really consider the notion that my time may have actually arrived. Reflecting back on the events of that night, I remember vividly asking the Lord to prolong my life so that I might have more time with my sons. Fully comprehending that I was actually dying, the single most important things to me had been my sons. I knew they needed more help from me—each with his own particular needs. At that moment of truth, I saw a lot of shortcomings in my life and realized how badly I wanted to be with them and help them avoid the kind of mistakes I had made.

A doctor came running out to see what all the shouting was about. He took one look at me and immediately began shouting orders in Chinese. Instantly I was whisked away to an emergency room bay. Almost immediately the doctor seemed to comprehend the problem and ordered nurses and orderlies to start intravenous medications. I remember him shouting at me that my heart was nearly stopped and he would have to give me a shot of adrenalin. He said I would feel nervous, but it was imperative to get my heart going. It's funny that I remember him yelling that to me because by this time I was pretty much out of it.

When I awoke, I was totally disoriented. I was in a huge room about the size of a high school basketball gymnasium. There were wall-to-wall gurneys occupied by Chinese people. As I regained my senses and looked around, I realized that every eye in the room was gazing at me. I could have supplied Webster with an excellent definition of paranoia for his new dictionary. I felt too miserable to talk, so I just put my head back down and went to sleep. A physician woke me up some time later and explained to me that I had nearly died and would have to stay in the hospital for several days to make sure I didn't have a relapse.

About that time, Nasim showed up. I told him to get me a taxi. He was astonished. As much as he reasoned with me, I refused to stay. The doctor was now arguing with me vehemently. All to no avail. He had explained there was really nothing more they could do for me, they just wanted to monitor things for a few days. I'm really not that ornery of a person. I just didn't see the value of lying around a room full of people staring at me for three days. I felt I could do much better in the comfort of my New World Center hotel room.

The Lord decided to prolong my life that day. That is proof enough for me to believe he really is there and he cares about keeping families together.

SIERRA LEONE

SIERRA LEONE, WEST AFRICA

Thanks to Aunt Geneva, I started a stamp collection when I was very young, determining that I would visit all the countries I had collected stamps from. Sierra Leone happened to be one of those countries, and so I went when the opportunity presented itself. I was primarily interested in gold, but I was told there was more value in diamonds by far, and I should focus my interests there. I had bought some gemstones in 1971 on a trip to Mexico, and I had been interested in them ever since. But still, my interest at the time was in gold. I made the arrangements and bought the tickets and was off to the embassy of Sierra Leone in Washington, DC.

No one was allowed to get a visa without personally showing up at the embassy and having an in-depth interview to determine why he or she wanted to go to Sierra Leone. That should have been my first clue. . . . At any rate, I passed the interview and was given a visa.

While I waited for them to prepare the visa, I went on a sightseeing tour of Washington, DC. I was fascinated and humbled by all the monuments and what they stood for. The most impressive to me was the Lincoln Memorial. All the others were wonderful, but there was something special that the artist had captured in the statue of Lincoln. As I wondered about what would be waiting for me when I got to Sierra Leone, I knew that whatever it was would be very different from what these statues represented.

My first stop after Washington, DC, was London. From there, I went on to Brighton, a city located on the south coast of England. Once there, I met a man who was related to a member of London Gold Market Fixing

Ltd. He was one of the five men who set the world gold price twice a day. He gave me the name of a Lebanese merchant, whom he said I should contact if things went bad or if I got into trouble. Clue number two.

After leaving London, I flew to Paris, where I changed planes and went on to Gambia in Northwest Africa. Then finally I got to Sierra Leone. I arrived in the early morning and was met by three men, Eyo, Madieu, and Abu. We exchanged introductions and pleasantries, after which Abu said, "Lay we go."

I just looked at him and stared. "What?"

He repeated it again, "Lay we go."

He then looked at me, furled his brow a little, and moved his head back as if to say, "What don't you understand about 'Lay we go'?"

After talking back and forth several times, they explained to me the native language was Creole, a combination of many native languages and influences, mixed with English. What he was trying to say was, "Let us go." However, in the Creole version of "let us go," or "let's go," it had been rendered as "lay we go." So after our communication finally cleared up, we drove down to the ferryboat that would take us across the bay to Freetown, the capital. It was so culturally fascinating and foreign that I felt as if I were walking through the pages of a National Geographic magazine.

I thought this might be a good time to visit the Lebanese merchant my acquaintance in Brighton had mentioned to me. After all, if I did need to contact him, I didn't want to have to go through introductions in a moment of crisis. I checked into the hotel, arranged another meeting with my contacts, and went in search of the Lebanese contact. I found his shop in the center of the commercial district. It was in a two-story, wood-framed building. I had a good visit with him, and I felt a lot more secure after our conversation. He was no pussycat; he had been around the block a few times. He laid things out in such a way that I developed a very good understanding of what he was telling me regarding the risks and dangers and how to stay safe in Sierra Leone, which was no small task. More importantly, he told me how to contact him in case of an emergency and where I could go for safety.

If I did run into any trouble, I knew this was a crucial connection to have. After we finished our meeting, I went downstairs to purchase a couple of items that seemed essential for my trip to the Sierra Leone interior. I placed the items on the counter, asked for the price, and reached into my pocket for the money. At that very instant, the loud speakers proclaimed prayer time and the cashier closed the cash register, spread out his bamboo mat on the floor, and knelt down to pray. In the Muslim world, they have prayer five times a day. It doesn't matter what they're doing when the speakers announce that it's prayer time. They put their forehead on the ground and start their prayer. I tried to speak to the cashier, but he wouldn't acknowledge my presence. There wasn't anything I could do so I departed, leaving the man to his worship.

I walked up to the city's main outdoor market where my culture shock hit a new high. The women wore brightly colored clothing, giving the market a very National Geographic feel. It takes a while for a Westerner to get used to the local customs. I was engrossed in the vast array of fruits, vegetables, and handmade articles that were unlike anything I had ever seen before.

Suddenly, loud voices caught my attention. People were yelling about a block down the street to my right. The noise grew rapidly louder, and soon a large crowd appeared with a very frightened young man in his early twenties firmly in their grasp. Several people had a good hold on him and were roughly shoving him forward. Men, women, and children were hitting, kicking and spitting on him from all sides. Everybody was yelling, "Tief! Tief! Tief!" (thief). The mob, now in a central location in the marketplace, was getting more agitated by the moment. They were completely out of control! The ferocity of their blows increased. The young man was bleeding and had a look of absolute desperation on his face. Just at that moment, when it looked like the crowd would beat him to death, several police appeared on the scene.

Most thieves have a natural aversion to policemen. This young man, however, was in tears. He had a distinct look of relief on his face. The policemen had just rescued him from a very dangerous situation that had been on the verge of costing him his life. With the poverty in Sierra Leone, stealing is a serious crime, and can easily cost a thief his life. It was quite obvious that people were frightened of the police. I had the impression they regularly took the law into their own hands to extract the justice they deemed necessary. They obviously weren't getting the justice they wanted from the government. As a matter of fact, for them the government was a mortal enemy.

After a couple of weeks, I began to develop a much deeper apprecia-tion for what the Lebanese merchant could do for me, as well as what he could do for people in other countries. One key thing he could do was to furnish an end-user permit. That was, in essence, a permit to legally, and I use the term loosely, own or store hardware and munitions for military purposes.

Let me illustrate exactly what I mean. I'm not a gambler, but for lack of something better to do one evening, I walked down to a casino on the beach. There were a number of Europeans there and two or three American sailors. They were drinking freely and were very friendly. I asked what they were doing in Sierra Leone. One of the men told me they were there with their ship, which was anchored in the harbor. As the story of the ship unfolded, it turned out that it contained huge quantities of foreign aid rice given by the United States government for the people of Sierra Leone. The man told me the president of Sierra Leone, Siaka Stevens, had sold the rice to the Ivory Coast. They were just waiting for another week before delivering the product.

I was astonished! How could the president sell the rice that had been given to the people of Sierra Leone? The people were starving and desper-ately needed the rice. They told me that it was just the way business was done in West Africa.

Later that evening, I met an English helicopter pilot—the personal pilot of Siaka Stevens. He informed me that the people would undoubt-edly riot when the ship left without unloading any rice. He said that Stevens would claim that he spoke to the spirits in his dreams when there was trouble with the people, and the spirits would tell him to send his sol-diers out to kill some people to settle things down, which he regularly did. He explained to me that their military had weapons, but no ammunition. The only ones that had any ammo were from Stevens's personal cadre of about one hundred fifty soldiers. With not only the possibility but also the likelihood of assassination and coup attempts, this was the only way Stevens could devise to have any degree of security at all. What a strange place! There was no security, no way to predict the future. Despite it all, there was plenty of gold to be found at very good discounts, and that was alluring.

During the next several months, I made numerous profitable trips, leaving my family for periods of time out of necessity. I was getting to know quite a few people, and I frequently had groups coming to me who were interested in doing business since I had the lay of the land. One afternoon, a very short man dressed in dark, brown robes with a matching turban showed up wanting to talk to me about doing business. He introduced himself, but I didn't know him and had never heard of him before, which was a red flag in this business. I explained that I needed references before I could have any serious discussions with him. He gave me the name of a man I knew quite well, and I told him that if he would bring that man back with him, I would be happy to discuss doing business.

He asked how much I knew about diamonds. I told him I knew very little and that my focus was on gold. He just smiled and walked away. Later that afternoon, he showed up with our mutual acquaintance he had mentioned earlier. He told me he wasn't interested in the gold business, but only in uncut diamonds. My response was that I couldn't help him because of my lack of experience and contacts in the diamond world. He just smiled again and asked if he could use the bathroom. I motioned for him to go ahead, and he went to the bathroom for about five minutes.

When he came out, he produced several folded sheets of paper from inside his robes. He laid them out on the table and unfolded them one by one. Inside the folded packets, there were piles of thousands of carats of rough diamonds, all laid out in the open on the table. This little man looked like he had no idea where his next meal was coming from, but inside his robes was a fortune in diamonds.

Again I protested that I didn't understand the diamond business well enough to be risking my money for them, but he claimed there would be no risk on my part. I asked how that could possibly be. He said I could just take the diamonds when I went to Europe and sell them. Anything over an agreed upon price would be mine to keep. I asked him how he thought he could trust me, considering he didn't even know me. To this, he laughed and said, "I know you very well." Somewhat befuddled, I asked him to explain himself.

"In our group," he said, "we know everybody in the business here, and you have established a very good name for yourself. Listen, you don't have to pay anything for the diamonds. Take them, and sell them at the best possible price. Then pay the owner of the diamonds an amount that is less than the agreed sales commission that we retain. You have no risk of losing profit whatsoever."

I felt a combination of flattery, suspicion, and disbelief, but after some more discussion, I agreed to do it. Fortunately, things worked out well. I made several trips and started learning a lot more about diamonds and the diamond business. And one thing I learned was that Sierra Leone was known for producing some of the best diamonds in the world, and there were a lot of them. I also learned that diamonds were much easier to travel with than kilos of gold—I liked that.

There was still one problem that continued to bother and gnaw at me. That was the unrest of the people. I was bothered by the fact that the president sold their food. It took one large bag of rice to feed a family of four for approximately one month. Rice is the staple of their diet, so it is very important to them. Sure enough, the helicopter pilot who I had met in the casino turned out to be right. Within a week or so of the ship's departing, word got out that the foreign aid rice on board the ship in the harbor had been sold somewhere else, and the ship was leaving. The people were hungry, desperate, and very angry. My fears were realized. The people began marching in the streets, protesting against the president's actions. I somehow had another brief, chance encounter with the president's helicopter pilot. He told me to get out of sight and lay low, as things were about to get really hairy. The president had spoken to the spirits again, and people were going to die.

It had certainly seemed a little melodramatic when my acquaintance in Brighton had told me about the Lebanese businessman, but he seemed like a good friend to have now. People were marching arm in arm in the street, directly toward soldiers who were firing at them. Rather than running, they continued marching forward. Only a people suffering with severe hunger and extreme desperation would march into the face of certain death as they did.

But even beyond the large confrontations like that one, there were random, individual killings all over the city. I recall one day when I had ventured out of my hotel to send a telex to the man in England. I hadn't gotten very far when I saw a teenage boy, who, not having the seventeen cents bus fare, had been thrown under the bus. He was lying lifeless in the middle of the street, a large cascade of blood from his crushed skull tricking down the street.

When I got back to the hotel, the manager called me over and told me that someone from the Sierra Leonean government had called to tell him that if Mr. Hamby tried to send any more telexes, or any other type of communication, he would be incarcerated. All air traffic had been stopped, railroads and highways had been blockaded, and only government-authorized communications were being permitted. I was a little terrified to think that anyone in this government knew the name of "Mr. Hamby."

I wanted to be as far away from these crazy people as I could get. I had seen enough during my visit to know there was absolutely no security. It wasn't like you could wave your passport and say, "You can't hurt me. I'm an American citizen." You couldn't say you were a citizen of Sierra Leone, or Germany, or England, or any other country for that matter. The status quo had digressed to anarchy in the blink of an eye as soon as the people discovered that the foreign aid rice had been sold and transported somewhere else.

While this trip had been very challenging, it was not without its moments of humor. At one point, I wanted to buy some gold and diamonds from the interior, but it was hard to get through all of the military roadblocks along the highways. I had been counseled to take someone with connections to the government to get through these roadblocks. When it came time to go, a short man, whose head didn't come up to my chest, was introduced as our political intermediary. He was short and boisterous. He had such a strange personality that it was against my better judgment to go with him to the interior. However, I didn't really have any other options, so I gave my nod of approval, and off we went.

We traveled for some distance in the interior before coming to our first roadblock. The men were all armed with submachine guns. They were acting very upset and nervous. There was a lot of yelling. Any sudden movement or miscalculation on our part, I'm sure, would have resulted in open fire. All of the sudden, to my extreme surprise, my short friend began to shout at the soldiers. I was shocked! I expected the guards to fire at any moment.

He screamed, "What's the matter with you morons? Are you completely stupid? Can't you see I'm a politician? Lower those weapons and open this gate right now! I'll report you!"

I could almost feel the bullets tearing through my body and imagined the other bodies being tossed backward with the force of the slugs. However, instead of shooting us all to pieces, to my utter astonishment, they began to apologize and opened the gate. I have never been so surprised and happy in my entire life! This little man turned out to be one of the most amazing individuals I had ever met. He was also a natural comedian like you can't imagine. The funny thing about it was he didn't mean to be. It was just his nature and the way he did things. He kept things on a light note during the entire trip.

My experiences with that man weren't the only times I laughed. I had been informed that in a village near the place we were traveling to, there was a man who had large quantities of gold for sale. We went to the village, which was more primitive than any place I had previously seen. This man lived in an enormous two-story, thatched-roof hut, which was good because he had five wives and forty-three children. He was highly respected in that area because he was the local *Haj*, or spiritual leader.

We were discussing a number of subjects and somehow got on the topic of men landing on the moon. He jumped out of his chair, screaming that I had blasphemed by claiming that man had landed on the moon. It took some serious talking to get him to the point that he wouldn't have his men skewer us. As we walked into another room, I just about fainted. There were half a dozen or more two-liter size earthen pots stacked to the top with gold nuggets. I had a rush of excitement. Given the man on the moon ordeal, I thought this uneducated man would have no idea of the value of gold. When I asked if he was interested in selling, he replied, "Sure I would be interested in selling it. How about we verify the second London fix and use that as a selling basis?"

I was so embarrassed! I think it had been obvious to everyone there that I thought I could buy the gold for practically nothing. The joke was on me. From that, I learned to never underestimate people.

This trip to the interior had taken two days. Suffice it to say, by the time I finished the trip and made it back to Freetown, I was grateful for anything that even remotely resembled cleanliness and comfort. This was mostly because I had eaten very little of anything throughout the whole course of the journey. Up to that point in my life, it was the worst food I had ever seen.

Since I'm one of those guys who can adapt almost anywhere if fed well, it should tell you something about the cooking in Sierra Leone that I never really did adapt there. That was always a sad thing for me. Sierra Leone is an otherwise beautiful country, with beautiful beaches. It had, at one point, enjoyed a substantial tourist business. I was staying in a French hotel that had catered to the industry. It was located right on the beach. The head chef was gifted, and during the days that we were barricaded in the hotel, we enjoyed excellent food. It would have been better if we hadn't known that the mobs, or these demons from the government, could break through the doors at any time and take whomever they wanted as prisoner—or just kill them outright.

During the two-day trip away from that hotel, I had developed a severe stomachache that had gotten progressively worse. By the time I got back to Freetown, I had to go to the hospital immediately. After an exam by the doctor, it was determined that I had a severe case of diverticulitis and needed surgery immediately. Diverticulitis occurs when small pouches form on the exterior wall of your large intestine rupture, and then become infected. The doctor explained that any one of these tiny perforations of my intestine could cause peritonitis—followed by a painful, miserable death. The doctor, who had been trained in the West, looked me squarely in the eye and told me to go back to my hotel, look in the mirror, and say to myself, "I am not sick. I do not need an operation. I am fine." Then I was to get on the very next plane back to the States and get the operation. He explained that, while he was a well-trained surgeon, if I were to be operated on in this hospital, I would certainly die of infection. Apparently, chickens scurrying under the beds were a bad thing in hospitals.

The hotel manager had a ham radio set up, and called to someone he knew in the Ivory Coast to make arrangements for a plane to touch down at the airport the following day. He explained that the plane would touch down at a certain time, and we had better be on the tarmac running after the plane with our bags if we wanted to get out of Sierra Leone. Arrangements were made for a truckload of armed soldiers to take us to the airport.

Once we were there, running for that airplane, some airport official demanded I empty my pockets and show my documents. Under the circumstances, I was really annoyed. I happened to still have some American money on me. When I took the bills out of my pocket, he tried to grab them away from me. Without even thinking, I just slapped the man in the face as hard as I could! The frustrations of the entire experience climaxed at that moment. I must've done a pretty good job because rather than retaliate, he just looked down and didn't say a word. It was as if I had caught a child with his hand in the cookie jar.

Finally, after getting past airport security, I rushed onto the plane and rejoiced that I was alive. I can't tell you how relieved I was when the wheels lifted off the tarmac. It was a long, circuitous route to get back to England; however, after visits to Liberia, the Ivory Coast, Mali, Gambia, and France, I finally made it! And with that landing came a relieved sense of security and stability. I had the operation when I got back to Utah, and it was a great success, although not without consequences, as you may learn in another story—a sizable portion of my large intestine had to be removed. But within two weeks, I was really feeling very well. I had certainly learned some good lessons about being grateful for the blessings I had—like, for instance, my life.

PRISON POET

ORLANDO, FLORIDA

In the mid-nineties I worked for three years at the Orange County Jail in Orlando, Florida, teaching life management and employability skills to the inmates in the Horizon program. What an interesting experience that was. I taught fifty-four students in one large common area, and all of them had been sentenced to a year or so in the county jail. Some were serving county time after having completed their penitentiary time, and others were serving county time before going to the penitentiary. It was a job that I really enjoyed, but it was an incredibly difficult task to try to keep the attention of fifty-four very distinct and individualistic men on an everyday basis. As diverse as these men were, they all had one thing in common—none of them wanted to hear some middle-aged Sunday school teacher expounding on his theories about life, liberty, and the pursuit of happiness.

It took some time to get them going, but once they caught the vision of what they could do, they were very enthusiastic and committed students. There were several key events that finally motivated them to want to dig in and get something out of the program, but one thing that really got their attention more than anything else was what happened to Joe. Joe pretty much fit the profile of all the other students, with a couple of notable exceptions. One was that he laughed and smiled a lot and had a contagiously good attitude. The second thing that distinguished him from the others was his face. He had undergone a dozen or more operations on his face and needed that many more to try to restore his appearance to something other than that of the Phantom of the Opera. Because of his appearance, it was common to see people recoil when they first saw him.

93

Leading up to his time in prison, by his own account, Joe was a happy, middle-class working man with a wife, a couple of kids, a dog, and a mortgage. And like any other typical husband, he was often asked to run to the store to pick up eggs, bread, or the newspaper. But one day, Joe's story took a unique turn. He was on his way to 7-Eleven to pick up a newspaper and some milk when his life suddenly and dramatically changed forever: a drunk driver smashed into his car so hard it left him trapped in a mess of tangled steel. The car's battery was pushed up through the dashboard and leaked acid onto his face, horribly disfiguring it. Saying that he was fortunate to have survived the crash would only have brought Joe's objection and a comment of he being anything but lucky. His face been crushed and torn from the accident and disfigured by the battery acid, not to mention his numerous broken bones.

It was probably a good thing that he was in a coma for several months after the accident; otherwise, the shock from his injuries probably would have killed him. After regaining consciousness and some basic orientation, he came to learn that his wife thought he would never wake up from the coma. She had sold their home, divorced him, married another man, and then moved with his children to another state. One instant he was on his way to the store, the next waking up only to be told that his whole life had been ripped away from him. After hearing that story, it's hard to imagine that he could ever want to smile or laugh again, but he did. Before learning to be happy again, his life took a turn for the worse, if you can imagine that to be possible.

After much rehabilitation, frustration, and hopelessness, he was very, very discouraged. He was also broke and homeless. He took up living in an abandoned trailer near the edge of a lake north of Orlando. Because of the coarseness of his appearance, Joe couldn't find work and was still suffering from the effects of the accident. As he was homeless and broke, he fell into some minor problems with the law. One policeman in particular seemed to have made it his life's mission to torment Joe. He was so discouraged and frustrated with life that he took the policeman's torment as a motive for focusing his anger and hatred on him. Broken, discouraged, and hopeless, Joe lured the policeman into chasing him into the abandoned trailer where he was living. As the officer rushed through the door, Joe hit him over the head with a lamp. He grabbed the policeman's revolver and aimed it at him. As the officer stared down the barrel of the pistol, Joe was in a state of fury. He really had a desire to shoot him, but he couldn't bring himself to do it. Instead, he struck the officer several times and then chased him out past his patrol car. He emptied the policeman's pistol into the hood and radiator of the car. To make a long story short, he was convicted of assault and was in the Orange County Jail finishing up his sentence.

Understandably, he was concerned about what life would be like when he got out. He still needed a significant amount of reconstructive surgery and was anxious about what the future held for him.

In our class, I would often call on the students to read a story or a poem they had written, so I knew that Joe had a talent for writing poetry. One day, I gave him an advertisement I had found for a national poetry contest. He just laughed and said, "Do you think an inmate, who has been in the penitentiary and is now in the county jail, has any realistic chance of winning a poetry contest?" Jokingly I asked if his social schedule left time for poetry and encouraged him to enter anyway. He just laughed and started filling out the contest paperwork. It was a very active contest, and as I recall there were approximately three hundred thousand entries from all over the United States. He read the notice to the class and they all had a good laugh. And, of course, I was the only fool to actively encourage participation. They had a good time at my expense, but that was okay. It was a good diversion for them.

After a couple of weeks, Joe got a letter from the poetry contest. It said the entries had been cut down to one hundred thousand and his poem was still in the running. The class had quite a good time at my expense with that news. However, they weren't laughing quite as loud as they had been. A couple more weeks passed, and another letter came. There were now fifty thousand poems remaining, and Joe's was one of them. The class took the news very differently at this stage. The doubters were still the doubters, but I began to see some polarization. Some of the guys were nodding their heads, saying, "Why not?" When it got down to a hundred finalists and Joe was still in the running, it was a different ball game—everyone was now encouraging him and rooting for him. Then one morning, Joe came to class with tears in his eyes. He was not a finalist anymore. He was the winner. Joe, just a number at Orange County Corrections to most, was no longer just a number but the victor of a national poetry contest. This one lonely, broken soul, who had suffered so much for so long, had finally become somebody. And the fact that he was awarded a thousand dollars for his poem not only validated Joe's victory, but it also convinced the other inmates they could become winners too—could become somebody too. Needless to say, class participation jumped like never before. But it wasn't just the inmates who were affected by this turn of events. I was also reminded that everyone has potential, no matter how they may look or what their past may be like. Joe's story motivated me to help my students reach that potential as much as I could. I learned a lot working at the jail, but this lesson affected me the most.

THE MISSING FACTOR

AIRPORT IN BELO HORIZONTE, BRAZIL

I had been buying emeralds in the town of Teófilo Otoni in the state of Minas Gerais for a number of years and I always loved to go back there. I knew many people in the city and it was always a nice treat to be in this friendly environment. The hotel I stayed in, the Hotel Lancaster, was like a second home to me. They had an excellent restaurant and if I wanted something that wasn't on the menu, they would always try and accommodate me. And there was a wonderful older woman there who took care of my room. It was always immaculate, as were my clothes, which she washed.

I had settled on this city as a good place to buy emeralds because it was far enough away from the mines to have the illusionary price drop down and yet I could still get a good selection of goods to choose from.

I had originally talked to Allan about the emeralds. When I told him we could pay our expenses, give a large quantity to the orphans, and could still make some substantial profit, he just lit up.

Allan and I had several days to complete our buying and get back to Bahia to catch our flight back to the states. The problem was that the buying was going very slowly because there was a shortage of quality goods on the market that week. It was going to be difficult to buy the goods we wanted and make it in time for our flight.

We finally finished our buying and got to Belo Horizonte to catch a flight to Bahia. This was the long way around but the only way we could make it in the time frame we had available. We were at the airport trying to get on standby for a flight to Salvador. It was an evening flight and, knowing we were on standby, we arrived hours early to get the first spot on the waiting list. As the flight time drew nearer, I saw a politician come in and talk to one of the airline managers. I had seen this all before and it didn't sit very well with me. The seats were being given to the politicians even though they'd showed up at the last minute. I went up to the woman in charge of the airline and really let her know how unhappy I was with the situation. She just kind of hung her head down and didn't say much, knowing she was in the wrong. I'm sorry to say that the "pure love of Christ" wasn't pulsing very strongly in my veins at that moment. Even though we had been wrongly bumped by a politician, it was no excuse for me to scold the lady at the airline counter. We noticed a girl about eighteen or twenty years old trying to get on the same flight that we were trying to get on. She was sobbing her heart out because of a family reunion she wouldn't be able to attend if she didn't get on that flight. It apparently meant an awful lot to her.

There were no other flights going to Salvador that night so the only choice we had was to rent a car and drive all night through the mountains of Minas Gerais. The roads were very difficult and full of huge holes. It was a very dangerous trip. If we didn't drive, we would lose our tickets. We walked to the rental car counter and asked them if they had a car we could rent. We quickly filled out the paperwork, threw our bags in the car and took off for Salvador. We had gone less than a mile when Allan said, "Wayne, what would it hurt if we went back and took that girl with us to Salvador?" He has such a loving and charitable nature; people are deeply impressed when they're in his presence. I was glad for that. Everywhere we went Allan always touched the people's hearts, especially the kids. Whether he was giving out candy or caressing their hair, he has an incredible capacity for love.

The girl had been in such distress at the ticket counter and so little time has passed since we left for Bahia, we were certain she would still be there. I flipped a U-turn and went back to the terminal. The rental car people were surprised to see us back and wanted to know if there was anything wrong. I told them no. We were just looking for the girl who wanted to go to Bahia. Just about that time the woman I had chastised at the airline counter said the flight was ready to go, and they had two seats available. Allan, who doesn't speak Portuguese, or at least didn't until we found ourselves having to make flight arrangements and check in a rental car at the same time, took care of the car and I got the airline squared away. People were yelling and stressing. We were stressing a little too, but mostly just happy to be able to fly instead of having to drive all night over a very dangerous highway.

We were doing all this with the airline people jumping up and down insisting that we get on the plane right now. As all this was going on we were also trying desperately to locate the girl we had come back for, but she was nowhere to be found. I figured she must have been able to find a seat on the plane. As we were boarding, I looked at every face in every seat on that airplane, but the girl was not to be found. She wasn't there—she was the missing factor. Allan's charitable heart had bought us two seats on that flight. We didn't say much, but we both knew we had been wonderfully blessed and protected.

BABY'S BREATH

BAHIA, BRAZIL

E very day the children showed up at my house at the same time. Rain or shine, they were always there. They usually had tin cans or small buckets. The regulars were oftentimes joined by new faces, and when my family and I would ask them where they were from, the typical answer was somewhere in the interior of northeastern Brazil. The new ones were almost always staying in some transient camp in cardboard shacks on the outskirts of town. We would ask, "How did you hear about us?" None of the children ever seemed to know for sure. They just said they were hungry and had been guided. They had a feeling that if they came, they would be given something to eat. Of course, the regulars already knew that to be true.

During my daily walks, I'd visit these people in their portable *favelas* (slums), as the locals referred to them. I wanted to learn what was happening there. An American who has never been to a third world country cannot even begin to imagine what these camps were like.

Families lived in shelters slapped together of broken boards and cardboard. From an outsider's perspective, the situation looked hopeless, but the will to survive is strong in human beings. It's an instinct that makes us do things we would never consider doing under normal circumstances. If you've ever faced death, you can understand. It's amazing these families had the courage to face each new day and greet each new sunrise with enthusiasm.

Something inside drove them forward. I spoke to some of them to learn what had put them in these circumstances. Why were they and their families there? Where were they from? The stories were incredible.

Somehow amidst all the trial and tribulation, they had one thing in common: hope.

Hope for what? Hope for a better place, the promise of a new and improved life. Hope for a dream that kept them going. They had all escaped drought, famine, abject poverty, and the lack of any belief that it would ever get better there. Their destinations were different, but the goal was always the same. They believed the promised land was waiting for them. I wrestled with the idea of telling them the truth. For most of them, there was no promised land. What would be waiting for them in São Paulo, Salvador, Bahia, or any city was a cardboard shack under a bridge—if they were lucky. A black, plastic lean-to alongside an incredibly polluted stream, if they weren't.

I witnessed this hope firsthand one particular day. I was driving by the rented house the branch[1] used as a chapel when I noticed some people resting on the front porch. I stopped to talk to them. They were from a poverty-stricken area in the interior, an area that hadn't received rain for five years. They needed to go to Salvador, where they believed they could find a better life. One of them had a relative there, so there was some realistic reason for optimism. I initially considered giving them bus fare, but I worried they would use it for food and still not get to Salvador. Instead, I decided to take them myself. It was about a sixty-mile trip, so I could be back in a couple of hours. I hadn't really planned to take them, but the Spirit wasn't whispering, He was shouting, "TAKE THEM!" So I did.

They were astonished. At first, they didn't really believe it. I'm not sure if any of them had ever ridden in anything but a bus or a truck. I bundled the five of them and their meager belongings into my car and headed out onto the highway.

When we arrived in Salvador, I took them to the section of the city where their relative lived. I didn't have a lot of money with me, but I gave it all to them. Though it wasn't much in dollars, it represented a windfall for them when converted to *cruzeiros*. One of the two men, the one who seemed to be the leader of the group, took it with shaky hands. The others gathered around him and stared at the money.

The man had seen some challenging times and had impressed me as being somewhat hardened. But he was the first to start crying, and his wife and friend followed soon after. At first, he was so overcome with emotion he couldn't get the words out. When he did, he just kept saying "God bless you."

I'm happy to report He did.

It's with some concern that I recount that story. I don't want to do my alms in public. But I want you to understand that these people aren't a bunch of vagabond thieves. They're human beings with the same feelings you and I have. It's just their ability to execute their dream of living a peaceful life and being able to provide for their families seems to have slipped away. I've told you this to prepare you for what's coming next.

Time went by. I learned a lot about these people as I passed by their camps on my morning walks. My associates and I had our usual daily visits of homeless beggars at lunchtime and sometimes in the evening as well. The cooks knew to never turn hungry people away. I was struck with how little it takes to bring joy into someone else's life, and I never wanted to miss an opportunity to offer that joy. I've been blessed countless times in my life by the actions and words of others. When I think back on blessings I've sought from the Lord, almost invariably the answer to prayers, or blessings, has come from another person. The people who have been an answer to my prayers have also received blessings from our Father in Heaven. It's a win-win situation. You can't ever get ahead of God. His blessings come in many different forms, but I think the best one is peace. That "peace of God, which passeth all understanding" (Philippians 4:7). It is indescribable.

But most of the locals feared the beggars. They were viewed as desperate and regarded as incorrigible thieves. I soon learned that there was an auction of sick children among the *favela* dwellers. The winner of each day's auction would take that child with them and beg on the streets. The idea was to garner more sympathy so the handouts would be greater.

Here is where my next experience comes in. One afternoon, I parked the car and walked up the street to take care of some business. There were always errands to run in the city center. The street was crowded. There was a woman holding a child and supplicating passers-by for money. The child was emaciated worse than any child I had ever seen. I would guess he was about six months old from his facial features, but his body was skin and bones. He was a dark-skinned boy, and all he had on was a tattered little red shirt. No diaper or socks. Just that little red shirt. His eyes were partially rolled back in his head. Flies swarmed around his face but he never blinked.

I was immediately alarmed. As I drew nearer, I could see the child was nearly dead. A few questions to the woman solidified my fears. This was an auction baby—one who had been bartered for and used to collect money. My first instinct was to yell at the woman. I scolded her, but there was more pressing matters at hand. I hailed a taxi, paid the driver, and gave the woman funds to take the child to a nearby clinic to have him attended to. She vowed she would and left.

I was wrought with emotion and had to take some time to compose myself before I could continue on. I thought about my sons and how precious they were to me. Could I ever be in such dire circumstances that I would auction one off? I couldn't imagine so, but then I wasn't living in a cardboard shack, not knowing where my next meal would come from. This experience traumatized me.

I related the story to the man I was doing business with in the city. He was interested, but not moved. He had seen it all before. Being a merchant in the main commercial district in town, this type of spectacle was common to him. He counseled me not to get too emotionally involved.

Despite the counsel, my emotions still ran high as I walked. I wandered around the handicraft market trying to sort things out in my mind. As I walked along the mosaic sidewalk to return to my car, I looked up. What I saw first brought panic, then despair. The woman was back, still holding the child and still asking for money.

In that moment, I felt stronger emotion than I have ever felt. The child was dead. I can't really distinguish exactly what I was feeling. So many emotions flooded in, all to no avail. It was too late. The child was dead.

His journey was finished. He was home. Behind him was the short, cruel life he had clung to as long as he could. No more auctions, cold, or hunger. He was at peace now, safe at home in the arms of a loving Father.

NOTES

1.   A branch is a small congregation in the LDS church.

LUCKY LINDY

CUENCA, ECUADOR

I once went on a trip to Central and South America, which included going to the Panama Canal, Guatemala, Mexico, Peru, and Ecuador. It was an outstanding trip. It was especially exciting for me because I had only previously been to Mexico. At the time, I worked under the direction of Dr. Paul Cheesman at the Book of Mormon Institute, which was attached to the College of Religious Education at Brigham Young University.

I had started as a research assistant with Dr. Cheesman, but because of my interest in anything to do with the Book of Mormon, I spent more time working in the Institute than I did doing my studies. I went on a number of short trips around the Western states with the professor. He was extremely knowledgeable—and I was a sponge, soaking up every bit of information I could get. For my job there, I had been doing a lot of research which included an old, Catholic priest named Padre Carlos Crespi in Cuenca, Ecuador. He had a collection of artifacts that contained hundreds—maybe even thousands—of gold, silver, and stone plates. What made them interesting to me was that they had writing on them.

On this particular trip, Dr. Cheesman had two other traveling companions beside myself. One evening we all met at our hotel, had dinner, and made our plans for the coming days. The three of them wanted to go to Easter Island, which was a fascinating prospect. Under any other circumstances, I would have loved to go; however, I opted out of the Easter Island excursion in favor of Cuenca, the real center of my fascination.

Once in Cuenca, I was very anxious to go visit Padre Crespi and his collection and went very soon after my arrival. While there, I asked him if anyone had ever written about his artifacts. He said yes, a man named Erich von Daniken had visited his collection and written a book about his trip to the tunnels, which was where the artifacts had come from. The name of the book was *The Gold of the Gods*. Padre Crespi stressed that Mr. von Daniken had never actually been to the caves. Someone else had gone and given him the photos.

Padre Crespi gave me the name of a Juan Moritz, an associate of von Daniken, whose attorney agreed to meet me in Guayaquil. I gave him the phone number that he could reach me with, and we set up a meeting. It was kind of a strange meeting—held in an abandoned warehouse at midnight. Well, you know what they say: curiosity killed the cat. I had already given up several of my nine lives, but how do you resist an adventure like this? Ancient tunnels full of gold and artifacts, an eccentric and mysterious author, and then, just to top it off, a secretive meeting in an abandoned warehouse at midnight.

The warehouse was located, predictably, in a dark and foreboding neighborhood over on the east side of the city. I found a taxi that would take me there and asked the driver if he would wait for me once we got there, seeing as I had no desire to stick around that area once the meeting was over. He readily agreed to wait—he just didn't say for how long. Once we arrived and I stepped out from the cab, he was generating a cloud of dust and looking for fourth gear.

In spite of the fact that the hair on the back of my neck was standing on end (and that I was more than a little concerned for my safety), it was actually kind of a humorous situation. As it turned out, I was not quite as far-removed from the city as I had thought. I wandered around a nearby plaza for a couple of hours before the attorney finally showed up. During that wait, I wandered down the street a few blocks and found that there were still some stores open and a few people on the street.

Down one particular street, there was a small, general merchandise store. It was one of those stores that have one of everything for sale, including a plastic model airplane on display in the front window. Capering around on the street in front of it was one little boy that particularly interested me. He was slender and had on raggedy nylon shorts, a T-shirt, and flip-flops. He was obviously in his own little world and didn't seem to be aware of anyone else. He would gaze at the plane in the window from time to time. Each time he looked, it was like he was dreaming of flying it. He would spread his arms out like wings, bend his body forward, and with a blitzkrieg roar, strafe all of his imagined enemies into submission, and then land to the roar of thunderous applause.

He had the whole thing well choreographed and had undoubtedly practiced it countless times. At one point, he stopped in the middle of one of his air raids. What a tender scene. He was bowed forward, nodding his head up and down to the great applause he was receiving from those he had saved from the tyrants. He stopped his performance periodically and went to the window to look at the model plane. He would then start up and take off on another adventure, perhaps like Charles Lindberg when he flew nonstop across the Atlantic Ocean, earning the nickname "Lucky Lindy."

I went over to the store and called to the boy. He was a little bashful when he realized he was sharing his experiences with me without knowing it. I asked him about the airplane in the window, and watched his eyes widen, as he eventually understood that I wanted to buy the plane for him. He was so excited! He could hardly control his anticipation as I went inside and bought the plane. The last I saw of him, he was flying over a hill in front of the store on a flight of fancy. Yes sir, Lucky Lindy was on her way now.

When the lawyer, along with Juan Moritz, finally showed up, I was irritated for having waited so long. But we soon got minor issues resolved and had a good discussion. He said he understood how hard it was for someone to believe that these caves really existed, but, in fact, they did. He said if I could wait for two weeks, he would arrange an expedition to go together to see the caves. I told him that was very interesting for me, but my schedule just wouldn't allow for that much time for at least another six months. We exchanged business cards and agreed to talk again when I became available.

I've never been back to see for myself, but if I am ever in Ecuador again, going to the caves will be high on my list of things to do.

Meanwhile, Lucky Lindy is flying the friendly skies.

GLOWING PHANTOMS
OF THE SURF

SOUTH MEXICO

Four college kids, a Volkswagen bus, and a couple thousand miles remaining. We were hot, tired, sweaty, and a little discouraged about how much farther we still had to go from our excursion to Mexico City to our homes back in Salt Lake City. It was getting late in the day as we sped northward up the west coast of Mexico. As we drove along, we came upon a fruit stand, nearly passing it in the dim evening light. We all had the same idea at the same time. The car spewed dust and rocks as it ground to a halt along the side of the road. What could be better than a fresh watermelon on the beach?

The beach had a pleasant breeze and the water beckoned us. After Virl agreed to take responsibility for the car keys and we had negotiated for a watermelon, we headed down to the beach. There was a small village across the road and a few hundred yards away from the beach. It appeared to be just a simple collection of huts that were basically constructed of bamboo and palm leaves.

There weren't any people around us, so we were left alone on the beach—and that was exactly what we wanted. We had planned to feast on the watermelon by breaking it up with our hands, and then go swimming in the ocean to clean off the sticky sweetness and grimy sweat.

As we neared the water, I realized that the light of the surf wasn't just a reflection of the moon. Wherever a wave broke, the water became florescent and put off a very unusual but beautiful light. It was fascinating to watch.

One boy, Javier, had followed us from the village. He was a very nice young man with long, shoulder-length hair. He explained to us that his hair was so long because he had been very sick as a baby. As a result, his grandmother had made a promise to God that if He would spare her grandson, she wouldn't cut his hair until he was twenty-one. He was very helpful and very curious. This little village was located too far down the Mexican coast, away from any major cities, to attract tourists to any appreciable degree, so naturally we were something of an anomaly and he wanted to find out all that he could from us.

He explained that florescent algae known as red tide caused the glow in the surf. He said it wasn't the least bit harmful, but warned us to be careful of the riptide, which is a very powerful current that can spontaneously appear sometimes, then go away from the shore without warning. Once caught in it, you have to swim parallel to the beach to escape while keeping yourself from expending all your energy and drowning.

Finally, after the watermelon was picked clean, we waded into the red tide and marveled at the fluorescence of the breakers as the waves rolled toward the beach. It was really a captivating sight. We waded in, washing the watermelon off, replacing the sticky juices with red tide. We were frolicking around like a bunch of kids, having a good laugh at how we appeared with the florescent algae covering our bodies.

We hadn't really paid much attention when Terry had said he was going swimming; he was a strong swimmer and we trusted his expertise. We watched him swim away, but it was only for a few minutes before we went back to amusing ourselves with the algae. However, after thirty minutes of not seeing Terry, we were getting worried. We began looking for him up and down the beach, with the help of our new friend, Javier, but to no avail. We just couldn't see him anywhere. Javier returned to the village and alerted the villagers of our plight. Almost instantly there were dozens of people there to help us look. We were on unknown ground, far from home, and sick with worry over our companion's disappearance. We all thought back on the warning of the riptides and the thought of our friend being dragged away without a chance to warn us.

I felt alternating waves of embarrassment and guilt for having lost a companion. I don't how long it was, but after a period of time the villagers all wandered back home. The three of us were beyond distraught. At Virl's suggestion, we knelt down and prayed. Each of us took a turn and poured our hearts out to the Lord. We waited patiently, praying silently while we took turns praying vocally. We just wanted to know where he was so we could bring him to safety. We prayed he was still alive.

Nothing happened for a half hour. We were immensely burdened with the loss of our friend. Then a glowing apparition walked up out of the surf. It was Terry, covered in red tide! What a relief. Although we rejoiced, very little was said amongst us. Terry never told us much about his side of his near-death experience. We all realized what had happened, but little did we know of the test that was yet to come.

We were all mentally exhausted, but after the major scare we just experienced, we were ready to put on dry clothes and get going. We asked Virl to get the keys so we could unlock the car. He just quietly said, "I don't have them." We were now really concerned and wanted to know where he had left the keys. He thought he had left the keys on top of one of the tires, but there were no keys on any of the tires. We knew that time was of the essence, because the tide was coming in; the car was far enough down on the beach that the tidewaters might cover up part of or even the entire car. Javier ran to get some tools that we might possibly use to pry one of the doors open.

On his return, there were a number of people following him, including men, women, and children. I could imagine they were entertained by a bunch of algae-covered Americans who parked their car too close to the tide. The giggles and smirks on the faces of the villagers didn't offer much comfort. They said there was a truck coming next week and we could catch a ride then to a city big enough to have a dealership where we could get the key made. While I am sure they meant well, we didn't have a week to wait for a key; we were still cold and wet and just wanted to get in the car and get going. Meanwhile, Terry was prying open the wing window on the driver's side with the tool that Javier had brought to us.

He hadn't noticed, however, that Javier was accompanied by a lot of people from the village. When he looked up and all of a sudden saw all these people looking at his florescent covering all over him, it was such a shock that he pushed too hard and the wing window shattered. More and more people were arriving.

There were some chuckles and smiles from the villagers. With wry smiles they suggested that the phantoms of the surf had our keys. While it was nice of Javier to bring the locals to assist us, it was becoming more of a show for them than a rescue. Soon, with Javier's encouragement, they all wandered away back to the village.

Alone and not knowing what to do, we all decided to all pray. We each took a turn, asking the Lord to help us find our keys. We had already felt relieved that night when Terry made it back safely, so we knew that a few more prayers could help us find a set of keys. Virl was the last to pray, and he gave a powerful testimony along with it. We all sat there for a few minutes, meditating.

Suddenly, without a word, Virl got up and walked in a perfectly straight line forty or fifty yards down the beach. He paused and looked down, standing over one spot in the water on this vast beach during the dark hours of the night. He then knelt down and stuck his hand in the water, which was now several inches deep and carrying sand to cover everything on the beach. He swished his fingers back and forth in the water, and when he lifted his hand I nearly dropped to my knees as well. He had the keys. We were delighted and couldn't find the words to speak. We just stood there in awe of what we had witnessed. It was a miracle. There was no way we would've found those keys so quickly and directly. The gratitude, humility, and faith generated by such an experience is not so easily put into words.

One thing was for sure, though: our testimonies couldn't be challenged at that moment. There was a witness that was undeniable for each of us there. There was no doubt that the Holy Ghost had guided us. We made our way back to our car, piled in, and quietly drove away. From time to time we would look at one another with a small, brotherly smile and simply nod, picking off stray bits of algae.

RETURN TRIP

TEÓFILO OTONI, BRAZIL

The view from the hilltop was beautiful and serene. It was surrounded by steep hills that were all a deep, dark green. It struck me as a really strange place for an airport. I was waiting for the plane to arrive from Belo Horizonte. My destination was Rio de Janeiro, but it's one of those deals where "you can't get there from here." Teófilo Otoni is a relatively small town and the air service was on a ten- or twelve-passenger Banderante, an excellent prop plane. To get to Rio, you first had to go to Belo and then on from there by prop, or change to the big airport and go by jet.

Wayne (left) with his sons David (center) and Matthew (right) overlooking Rio de Janeiro.

I was relaxed and comfortable and in no particular hurry. In South America one of the most valuable lessons one learns is to not get agitated about things you can't change. You can rant and rave, but things have their own set pace. Honking, hollering, and swearing won't change anything. You know you're acclimated when you can comfortably go with the flow. I was going with the flow. The strange dichotomy of this scenario is that if the plane were on time, you better be ready and running or you'll be yelled at or left behind. It's actually pretty comical if you think about the contradiction.

The drive from Bahia had been challenging, but, as always, interesting. It was about a five-hundred-mile trip, all told: two hundred and fifty miles to Vitória da Conquista and then another two hundred and fifty to Teófilo Otoni. The first half hour is filled with magnificent stone boulders rising a thousand feet high with tropical pooling at the base. Children sold enormous snakes draped over their shoulders. The snakes were so large that they were dragged on the ground on both sides. Children also sold large iguanas or fresh-roasted cashews. Brazil is like a drive-thru flea market.

I drove most of the way at night, which greatly increased the difficulty and danger. The roads were narrow and winding and jammed with trucks. There were no railways in Brazil at this time, so the highways served as the arteries to supply goods to the nation. They always seemed to be overloaded and the cars labored greatly going up hills. It's an exhausting trip.

On this particular trip, I learned a valuable lesson about enduring to the end. With very hazardous and challenging roads and driving conditions, I had not only offered a heartfelt prayer before leaving, I was constantly praying as I drove. Once you pass Conquista, it's pretty much a downhill run, and that did make it easier. The trade off is that the roads are a lot narrower and have a million twists and turns. Actually, I was pretty famous in the area for one time having made the run in seven and a half hours. That was an aberration. There had been some kind of a national truck strike, the weather had been dry, and the road was in a good state of repair. I felt like Han Solo, but didn't push my luck like that again.

I breathed a sigh of relief upon arriving in Teófilo Otoni. I remember thanking the Lord for guiding me safely as I turned off the main highway and headed for the Hotel Lancaster. I had maneuvered the highway at night with a light rain, which on this particular road triggered some very treacherous road conditions. But after making it to safe ground in the city, I didn't have a care in the world. I was relaxed and happy in antici-pation of a nice hot bowl of soup at the hotel. I had been there so many times; it was like my second home.

I let down my guard and my good luck on the road ended all too soon. I had the right of way and wasn't paying attention. From the left, a red sedan came charging through a stop sign and smashed into the driv-er's side of my car. Glass flew everywhere and pelted me in the face. I had been jolted pretty hard; the whiplash affected my entire body, making it nearly impossible to move. Someone called the local abortion doctor, who happened to live nearby. The doctor came and picked the glass out of me, got me fixed up, and gave me a sedative and a muscle relaxer. By the time my body hit the bed in the hotel, I was out like a light and slept until noon the following day.

The lesson: Don't let your guard down until your mission is com-pleted and you're on safe ground. Endure to the end. Just because I had passed the five-hundred-mile marker without an accident didn't mean I was home free. I still had six blocks to go. And little did I know at the time, the most perilous part of the trip was still ahead.

The driver of the red sedan, a local attorney, had been pretty drunk when he smashed into my car. Someone from the hotel had come and made arrangements for me to visit him in a couple of days and settle things. He didn't have any insurance and I would have to get an estimate and then get the money from him. From what I learned of him, that could well be a formidable task. He was known as a shady character that had connections to criminals and oftentimes defended them in court. I wasn't looking forward to the meeting. The next day, the man from the hotel called and confirmed the time of my visit with the attorney.

I rested for a day and let the sedatives work their way out of my system. One of my favorite activities was to go for a walk in the park just outside the hotel. The commerce of the city is based on gemstones. I was well known in town, and when I walked through the park, nearly everyone I passed greeted me. I had bought stones from most of them. It was a good feeling, again, like being home. The *preguiça*[1] in the park were always fascinating to watch. The park also offered bags of fresh-roasted peanuts and popcorn.

Eventually, the time arrived for the meeting with the drunk driver. I walked the several blocks to his office. The outer gate was, as expected, closed. The custom in Brazil is to clap your hands when you want to get the attention of the person within. I clapped and waited. There was no response. I clapped again and waited. Finally, a man came out and opened the gate. He directed me in through the front door and then walked around the side of the building. It was obviously more of a workshop than an office. The attorney came in through a side room. He was holding a revolver and had my total attention. I was too far from the door to try and retreat.

He would either get rid of me or negotiate with me. I hoped for the latter. I was alarmed, but not panicked. I figured I knew too many people in the city for him to seriously consider shooting me. But then who can predict what an irrational man will do? All I knew was that a drunken man with a gun was walking toward me in a dimly lit workshop. He spent several minutes berating me for having been at the intersection when he wanted to go through it. With a sense of logic like that, what hope for rationality was there? He ranted, waving the gun and saying it wasn't really his fault and he shouldn't have to pay for the damage. The only sensible thing was to agree with him and leave.

I chose not to do that.

To this day, I can't explain why I chose not to leave. Maybe it was adrenalin. There was plenty of it flowing. Plus, I was outraged that someone could be drunk and cause an accident and then blame it on the victim. I could tell he was on the verge of losing self-control, and I needed to be very careful. He didn't want to pay, especially to some foreigner. He came menacingly close to me, waving the gun in an increasingly exercised manner. He was right in front of my face and speaking in a very loud voice. His breath reeked of liquor. That gave me some degree of hope. His reaction time would be slow.

Time seemed to freeze as I reached down and grabbed the gun from his hand. He offered little resistance. It was as if he had surrendered his will to mine. We were the only two in the room, but in some way I can't explain, I sensed there was someone else there, a spiritual presence there to accompany me. The attorney completely acquiesced and now spoke in a calm and rational voice. I kept the pistol at waist level, but not pointed at him. He said he had gone to the auto body shop and they had told him how much it would cost to repair the car. The figure matched the one they had given me. He took out his checkbook and started writing a check. My first instinct was to protest. At that moment, though, I felt a spirit of calmness come over me. I knew his check would be good. Nothing else was said. I took the check and left, depositing the weapon on the lid of a rusty drum.

On the way back to the hotel, I stopped at the Nordeste office to arrange my flight to Belo Horizonte. That was when the fear of the past events finally set in—the fear of what could have taken place. The owner, Presciosa, was amazed as I recounted my experience with the attorney. He said I was lucky to have gotten out with my life. He confirmed what I had heard about the attorney being a dangerous character. I wasn't prompted to give the details of the encounter or the feelings of a divine intervention. It wasn't important that he knew. It was only important that I knew.

At the airport, a gentle breeze was blowing as I searched the horizon for the arriving plane. There was nothing but occasional clouds. The small dirt runway airport was calm and peaceful. The events of the last several days were on my mind. How many times had I been spared by divine intervention? I was cognizant of many. There were undoubtedly countless others I was unaware of. Deep in thought, reflecting on the events of the trip, I was unaware of an arriving car until after it had pulled up close to where I was sitting. Two men and a woman bolted from the car, running to a small plane parked alongside the landing strip. One of the men, from all appearances, was a physician and the other appeared to be a pilot, hurriedly preparing the plane.

The woman was carrying a small child. The look on her face is permanently etched in the back of my mind. Something was very wrong. She had the most profound look of despair I've ever seen. The doctor helped her into the already running plane and away they went. I watched as the plane disappeared into the horizon. I hadn't noticed previously, but they had been accompanied to the airport by a police car. The officer was now telling a group of people the child had something stuck in his throat and they were desperately trying to get to a hospital in Belo in an effort to save his life. The medical services in Teófilo Otoni had serious limitations.

Having lost two children in infancy myself, my heart was breaking, and I struggled to choke back the emotion.

I realized at that moment that the events I had experienced this past week were very unimportant compared to the drama that had just unfolded in front of me. A human life, a child's life, was in the balance. Turning away from the other passengers and seeking solitude gave me the chance I needed to gain control of my emotions.

This innocent little spirit, sent here by a loving Father, was in trouble. I silently prayed, pleading with Heavenly Father for His help.

It was very quiet. No one was speaking now. I wasn't the only one to have been touched by the experience. The ground crew began wheeling the baggage cart toward the runway. The overdue plane was on the horizon and everyone was eager to go, gathering personal belongings in anticipation of the departure.

I guess everyone realized it at the same time. There was a plane coming all right, but it wasn't the Banderante. It was the small plane that had just taken off minutes earlier. No one said a word. The plane touched down and taxied up to the parking area. The passengers all got out, but this time they weren't in a hurry. Nor did they pause. There was no conversation as they walked back to their car. The woman clutched the little child's lifeless body. She wasn't sobbing. She was past that. It was a look that will haunt me forever. It was pure heartbreak far beyond my ability to describe, but which, from experience, I understood.

NOTES

1.   A *preguiça* is a sloth.

SPINAL MENINGITIS CURVEBALL

HOUSTON, TEXAS / NEW JERSEY

In the early 1970s, I started a pollution control business based in New Jersey, serving customers from Baltimore to Boston. I started originally cleaning large oil and chemical storage tanks and cleaning up oil spills, and eventually also moved into recycling chemicals. This was a great time to be in this business as an ecology movement was just getting started and strict enforcement was becoming a reality within the industry. As business developed, I concentrated more and more on recycling and ended up going to Houston, Texas, to discuss setting up a recycling plant and selling my company to a large corporation called Browning-Ferris. The negotiations had gone very well and there was a possibility that I could sell my company for a very large sum of money. They were interested in recycling, as that was a key tie-in to their business of disposing of garbage, which had a huge potential for generating BTUs and in turn for generating electricity. I had conceptually designed a facility for recycling oil and chemicals and generating electricity by burning garbage. The interest was keen on both sides.

I was accompanied on this trip by a chemist who worked for my company and was well versed in the goals we wanted to reach. We were very happy after the meetings for two reasons. The first reason was that they had conceptually accepted and endorsed the idea of the recycling facility, which I had proposed to build in South Jersey, and second, because they were talking in terms of three million dollars for my company. Of course, they had offered me a management contract. Actually, they had demanded I take an employment contract for three to five years with a very nice salary and numerous company benefits.

Needless to say, I was a very happy young man. The chemist and I went out to dinner and then back to the hotel. We hadn't been there very long when I began to have a terrible headache and felt like I had a fever, so I excused myself and returned to our hotel. I remember it was a Hilton Hotel, right in downtown Houston. It was a very nice hotel and came equipped with a scale in the bathroom. I was feeling worse by the minute so I took a hot shower, weighed myself, and went to bed.

I awoke sometime during the night, and was shocked at what had happened to my body. I was sure that the chemist had played a trick and dumped a bucket of water on me while I was sleeping. The sheets, the pillows, the covers, and my clothing were completely wet. I was confused because I was in the room all by myself and couldn't understand how the bed could have gotten so wet. Most memorable of all, though, I had the worst headache I have ever experienced. I was burning up with fever. A little internal alarm in my head told me that if I wanted to go home, I had better do it right now. Acting on the prompting, I showered, paid the hotel bill, and went directly to the airport and caught the first available flight for Philadelphia.

The flight had a stop in New Orleans and would go directly from there to Philadelphia. People were looking at me very strangely, and several of the stewardesses asked me if I felt all right. The pain in my head had become unbearable and I had taken several pain pills given to me by the stewardesses. When the plane arrived in New Orleans, I left the plane, telling the crew that I needed to find a hospital or doctor. I was placed in a small infirmary in the airport and waited for what seemed like a long time for a nurse to show up. She told me she didn't know what was wrong with me, but she knew that it was something serious and needed to be attended to by a doctor rather than a nurse.

With the nurse's help, I made arrangements for the next flight to Philadelphia. By this time, I could hardly function. Everything was getting black and closing in on me, and the pain had become even worse, which I hadn't imagined was possible. When I finally boarded the flight, it was nearly empty so I was able to lie down across a few seats and fall asleep. I didn't have any seat belt around me and wasn't cognizant of anybody speaking to me or even knowing where I was at. When the plane landed and the pilot engaged the reverse thrusters, I was thrown off the seat and onto the floor. The jolt woke me up, and under other circumstances it would have been really funny, but I felt so poorly I couldn't even function on my own. The airline people put me in a wheelchair and took me to where my wife was waiting, and then on to our car. My wife had an extensive background as a medical transcriptionist and recognized immediately that she had to get me to a hospital as soon as possible.

She took me to a clinic in Willingboro, where the doctor told her I had a bad case of the flu and needed to rest. He even gave her some sleeping medicine for me, and told her to have me sleep as long as possible. We went home and I got into bed, but I had been there for only an hour or two when I suddenly awoke with the absolute conviction that I needed to get to the hospital immediately.

By the time we reached the hospital in New Jersey, I was fading in and out of consciousness and I only remember glimpses of things that were happening. I vaguely remember a doctor with a German accent doing some initial tests and shouting to the others that I had spinal meningitis, and that they would have to put in a spinal tap immediately. He was shaking me and yelling at me, trying to get some information about where I had been and what medicines I had taken, but I was too far gone to be of any help.

Although I was sicker than I had ever been in my life and barely coherent, to this day I still remember vividly the penetration of the needle into my spine, about halfway up my back. It was as if the sound were being magnified. I can remember distinctly hearing a crunching sound as the needle penetrated into my spine.

The doctor explained to my wife, and later to me, that he thought it was, in all likelihood, too late to save my life, but he felt like he had to try. At first, he said that it was unlikely I would survive the night, and if I did, I would probably lose my sight and hearing because of the excessive pressure caused by the inflammation around the spinal cord.

She also learned through the airline employees and the hospital personnel that apparently three people had contracted spinal meningitis in Houston. One had died within hours in Houston, and an airline pilot had died within a day. Of course, I wasn't aware of these issues at the time because I was still mostly unconsciousness.

What happened next is very personal and very special, but very real and powerful to me. I was the only patient in my hospital room, which was large and had two beds, but the other one was unoccupied. I remember that I was on the opposite side of the room from my bed, floating, I guess you would say, in the upper corner, looking down on the room. I saw two missionaries in short-sleeve white shirts; they had their hands on my head, giving me a priesthood blessing.

I was told that I was unconscious for quite some time. I'm not sure how long, but I think it was at least some time the next day when I awoke alone in the hospital room. I felt terrible, but I knew I would be all right. I had an absolute certainty, notwithstanding the pain I was having at the time, that I would be all right and would have a full recovery.

I don't know exactly how or when it happened, but during the next few days and weeks I was given to know with an absolute certainty the things I needed to do. The big business deal I had been so excited about in Houston was no longer important. I came to understand that I was to give up that business and go back to Utah and attend school at Brigham Young University. Not only that, I also knew that I should major in journalism and even understood the specific classes I should take. These spiritual impressions I was given during this time were very specific and profound and were immensely valuable to me. But while my recent convictions caused me to rejoice in the Lord's plan for me at this time, they caused some serious strife to erupt with my wife and her family. My wife wanted the way of living that would come with that three million dollars—she had grown accustomed to it. She also didn't want to leave here family.

She and her family were all convinced that the meningitis had damaged my mind, and that I was acting completely irrational. They argued fervently that to walk away from the potential money that had been negotiated in Houston was an act of madness. I told them it wasn't a matter of money. The money didn't matter at all. I had been told to do something by the Lord, and I was determined to do it, no matter the cost.

Following the prompting, I sold my company and relocated to Utah. My wife and son would join me a year later. College was a difficult transition for me. I was only in my mid-twenties but I'd had a lot of success and wasn't used to living by the rules of anyone but myself. It was tough to do everything asked of me by my professors, to be disciplined by them. I was working toward my degree in communications with an emphasis in journalism, as I had felt inspired to do, but wasn't sure of the specifics as of yet.

One day I found myself standing in the BYU library, and I really wasn't sure why. I was drawn to look at the book Joseph Smith had used to translate the book of Abraham. The book contained numerous ancient characters and I was thoroughly intrigued, wanting to know more. Because of this experience and a prompting to visit Dr. Paul Cheesman, I began working with him in the religion department of the Book of Mormon Institute. In due course of time, I was awarded a chemical patent, opened a copper refinery in Arizona and then a gold refinery, which in turn led to my work in the gold industry, and finally my work in the gemstone industry. The Lord knows where we need to be and we'll only get there if we listen to the promptings, even if they come in the form of a spinal meningitis curveball.

MARATHON MAN

SALT LAKE CITY, UTAH

It is essential for people to know who they really are in order to be in a position of personal growth. Sounds pretty easy, right? But it's actually quite a challenge to find out and know for yourself who you really are and why you are here. To know if those things you absorb in your life reflect who you are. I would like to tell you about an experience I had trying to answer that question.

As described in the previous story, I had just barely survived a near-fatal struggle against bacterial meningitis, during which I had learned through inspiration that I was supposed to move from my home in New Jersey to Utah, giving up my extremely lucrative petroleum tank-cleaning business to study journalism at Brigham Young University.

During the weeks I was at home recuperating, I spent most of my time watching the 1972 Olympic Games. I had been on the track team in high school and was very interested in those events. I was particularly amazed to see a man, an American named Frank Shorter, win the gold medal in the marathon. It was hard to believe that a man could run 26.2 miles and sprint the last mile or so of the race. It seemed hard to comprehend that a human being could run that far. I determined that someday I would run a marathon. I was pretty sure it would be sometime in the distant future, given my present circumstances.

A lot of things happened during the ensuing seven years, but by 1979 my family and I had moved back to Utah, and I had decided that I would run the *Deseret News* Marathon in Salt Lake City on July 24, Pioneer Day—a Utah state holiday commemorating the original pioneer's first entry into the Salt Lake Valley. I had determined that I was going to run this race and nothing could stop me. I was completely dedicated, but I was also completely unprepared. I had spent a lot of time reading books and talking to people with marathon experience and had put together what I thought was an adequate training program. I had trained hard six days a week and was putting in about fifty miles of early morning runs each week—I was feeling great.

The closer it got to July 24, the more I realized I wasn't properly prepared. I really worked hard, but it became very evident as the date approached that I wasn't ready. I had dreamed about this since watching Frank Shorter in the Olympics, but I came to the realization that while dedication was absolutely essential and necessary, it was only of sufficient value when combined with preparation; proper, methodical preparation. I agonized over it for days and thought a lot about it during my morning runs. In fact, that was the only thing I thought about. I concluded that if I didn't finish what I had started, I would never have enough self-confidence to ever do anything of importance in my life. I had prepared the best I could and determined that I would let willpower and my reliance on the Lord's mercy do what they could and just hope for the best.

On July 23, I prepared the things I would need for the race, and went to stay at a motel in Salt Lake so I wouldn't have to get up so early on race day. Because of the hot summer days, the race started at 5:30 a.m. to give the runners a jump on the sun. I parked my car in Parley's Canyon and walked to the golf course where the race was to start. The *Deseret News* Marathon was known among runners as one of the more difficult distance runs in the United States. It was not only 26.2 miles long, but it was at a high elevation, with steep uphill and downhill portions of the course. The uphill portions are difficult and challenging, but the downhill parts are even worse because of how they beat your body. Due to the difficulty of the course, there were less than a thousand runners. That's relatively modest for a marathon, but when you're in the middle of the stampede, it seems like there are thousands of runners.

The starting official fired his pistol and away we went. There were so many people jockeying for position, everyone trying to get a step ahead. There was one particular man who seemed to be obsessed with getting out of this initial pack. He had a kind of faraway look in his eye and was uttering animal-like sounds as he grabbed arms and shoulders trying to pull himself forward. The people he was affecting complained at first, but when they saw the desperate look on his face, they just let him be. The group was out of the golf course now and the pace quickened as we were on a gradual downhill slope. We had gone only a short distance when the man let out a yell of desperation as he fell to the ground. He hit very hard. It was an awful sound. One of the runners who had been grabbed by him said, "Looks like old Darwin was right."

Wayne running in the 1980 Deseret News *Marathon.*

For everybody who was running, this was a serious endeavor that had taken many months and miles of training to prepare for. The fall and subsequent comment by the runner was a counterpoint that brought forth a kind of reaction that was unexpected. Everyone laughed; some so hard they had to temporarily stop running. The comment, though harsh for the man that fell, and humorous for those who heard it, I'm sure caused everyone to reflect on their limitations, and realize the human frailties inherent in each individual.

Given the other runners' reactions to the incident and their subsequent comments, it was obvious that no matter how great the bravura, each runner determined his own mortality, his own experience here on Earth, and how he would go through it. The first few miles of a marathon probably wouldn't have a runner questioning himself about such weighty matters. But by the time he gets to about twenty-one miles, he is very much aware of the frailties and limitations of his mind and body. At that distance, a runner "hits the wall." From there to the finish line, his body just doesn't want to cooperate. It is simply a challenge of mind over matter. Your mind has to convince your body to take you to the finish line whether it wants to or not. And believe me, at twenty-one miles your body won't want to take another step. At least, that was how I had broken the challenge down from reading books and talking to runners. Up until the time of this marathon, I hadn't run more than ten miles at one given time. There was a lot to learn and the lessons had begun.

The course broke down roughly as follows: the first half to one mile in the golf course was uphill. The next several miles were a moderate downhill followed by a moderate uphill of five or six miles. Two or three miles of downhill followed that. Next were a couple of miles of moderate to steep uphill. Then the worst part of all—several miles of very steep downhill. This is the worst because of the punishment your body takes with the downhill jolts at every step. Some miles of much-needed gentle downhill followed that with a moderate downhill to the end of the course. As I said, it is an extremely difficult course. And while runners may shy from the brutality, they yearn for the challenge.

I knew from my training, and from the endorsement of many runners, that the brand of shoes I was wearing were the very best on the market at that time. Runner's World magazine said that it was flat out the best shoe on the market. I knew that shoes were very important and necessary to give me the support I would need for such a long race. The shoes were great, but I had forgot one very important detail—to not run a marathon in new shoes. The shoes felt good, but I had a pronounced pain in my right foot. My right ankle had been badly damaged with torn ligaments five different times. In 1968 I had undergone an operation to put that all back together. Afterwards, the doctor told me the operation had been a great success. He further explained that I shouldn't have any more trouble tearing ligaments, but I would never be able to run again and would always walk with a pronounced limp. Well, thankfully, that turned out to be incorrect.

The shoes felt good until the first downhill stretch. At that point, they were getting uncomfortable because my foot was sliding forward in the shoe. It had started to get very uncomfortable when I came to the steep uphill portion of the race.

With the pressure taken off my toes in the front of the shoe it felt much better. Now was the first really terrible part of the experience. Dropping down from the top of the hill into Immigration Canyon was a very steep drop. My toes were banging against the front of the shoe and I felt a lot of pain. It didn't take long to find out what was happening. I could feel my toenails were being hammered out of their place by the constant pounding. The question was, should I stop and end the suffering or should I go on? Dedication and preparation were on my mind in a big way. Nobody had ever told me you could lose toenails on a steep downhill if you didn't have your shoe properly fitted and broken in.

I was trying to stay hydrated. It had gotten very warm and everybody was sweating profusely. I had a tendency to sweat more than normal and had to be careful not to miss any water stops. Most runners would try and drink while they were running and end up spilling most of the water or Gatorade. However, I would stop for five seconds to ensure that I got a good amount inside me.

I came to a rest station near Hogle Zoo, and some workers just looked at me and grimaced. My feet or toes were starting to bleed. Somebody pointed to my chest. I looked down and was surprised to see blood coming from my chest. Nobody had told me you should tape up your chest before a long-distance race. Just the irritation of your shirt rubbing up and down against your skin thousands of times during a race will rub the skin away and you'll start bleeding. And of course you'll have an abundance of perspiration running into very sensitive open wounds. And as if that weren't enough, I realized the top of my legs had been rubbing together and I didn't have the experience to know that I should have put Vaseline there before the race to cut down the friction.

I took pity on the spectators and ran through a couple of sprinklers and tried to clean myself up, but I was still a mess when I crossed the finish line.

When I crossed the finish line, I jogged off to an area apart from the crowd, where I had some very special moments with my Father in Heaven. My feelings were tender and there were tears, not of sadness, but pure joy. I had come to understand a lot of things about myself during those 26.2 miles. This marathon was like an outline of my life. I could see so many times when I had started things with the best of intentions, but not with the best preparation. Realizations and information seemed to be flooding into my mind.

This event had taken a lot of my time and dedication, and it would take some more time to comprehend all the things I was seeing and feeling. One special thing I remember reflecting upon was that the Savior shed far more blood than I had, and suffered infinitely more than I ever would, all for the accomplishing of a particular goal. What he achieved was infinitely greater than what I had, but I had at least gone through my own, microcosmic version of a similar process. It brought the reality of his sacrifice closer to home, deeper in my heart.

DARK CANYON

SOUTHEAST UTAH

What did I know about Dark Canyon? Nothing, really, except what I had been told by a retired man I had become acquainted with at the Provo Temple. I had been making trips to Latin America, visiting the ruins of ancient cultures. I was examining any possible relationship of the Book of Mormon to help increase my understanding of its teachings. When I told my friend about these trips, he was very interested and told me of similar trips he had made down into the bottom of the Grand Canyon.

He told of having discovered a cave in the bottom of Dark Canyon, one of the major side canyons that join into the Grand Canyon. He and his companions had decided that giants had inhabited the cave. I asked how he had come to that conclusion, and he said the table and chairs that had been carved out of the wall of the cave were enormous and would have been far too big for any normal-sized human being. He said when he had sat on the chairs he was dwarfed as if he were a child. They had also found pieces of broken pottery and various artifacts in the cave, but the large fixtures were by far the most interesting things there.

Don't ask me how I made the connection between giants in the bottom of the Grand Canyon and the Book of Mormon, but within a few days I was on my way to Dark Canyon. When you're young and adventuresome, you don't need much prompting to go off on some new adventure. I made the journey with two friends who had previously accompanied me on similarly themed trips to Mexico. We headed out with a pickup truck, a two-man nylon pup tent, rope for repelling down the canyon walls, and food. The weather was pleasant the day we left, so we foolishly didn't bother to check the forecast. If we had, we could have saved ourselves a lot of grief.

We drove past Hanksville, Utah, and then cut cross-country in an area that had no roads but afforded us the closest entrance to the rim of Dark Canyon. We crossed some very rough terrain in our four-by-four pickup. It was quite late when we arrived at the edge of the canyon, so we got into our sleeping bags and spent the night there. We awoke in the morning enthused about beginning our descent to the cave. We had our breakfast, packed up our gear, and headed for the canyon rim, which was maybe a mile away. The terrain was fairly level, but rough, and there were a lot of rocks and trees.

The descent was fairly easy at first, but it got much more difficult the deeper we went into the canyon. We left rope for the return trip at a few places along the way. There were a couple very difficult places where we had to use rope just to get down to the next level. It was very steep, and several large rocks we dislodged made quite a racket as they descended through the trees. Although the descent was treacherous, I thoroughly enjoyed myself. The canyon was beautiful. I paused occasionally to verify our position on the map by comparing it to the physical characteristics of the canyon.

It was about midday when we arrived at the bottom, and the canyon took on a whole new life. A feeling as dark as the canyon's name permeated the chilly air. We decided to split up and see if we could find the cave of the giants. We covered a lot of ground during the day, but didn't find anything resembling a cave. As the day grew later and later, a light rain began to fall and the air became even colder. It was way too late to think about trying to climb back up the canyon wall, so we each set out to find dry wood to build a fire and get us through the night.

The temperature neared freezing, and exposure was a genuine concern. I was completely exhausted and found a relatively dry spot on top of a large rock to lie down and take a quick nap. I immediately fell asleep.

I'm not sure how long I slept, but I awoke to a shocking sight. One of my companions was standing over me with a large tree branch raised high above his head, ready to bring it down on my head. His eyes were dark and an evil look covered his face. I jumped up, confused and fully awake.

"What do you think you are doing?" I yelled, panicking.

He shook his head a little and blinked his eyes before responding. "I was just trying to give you a little fright," he said. His face went from evil to confused. He wasn't acting himself.

"Well, it worked," I said. That kind of trick would be typical among friends out in the wilderness, but the look on his face put it in a different category for me. I felt a strange spirit in that canyon, kind of a heavy, brooding spirit.

When our other friend joined us, he was angry and argumentative. I suggested we immediately start our preparations for the night for practical reasons, but also to dispel the spirit of contention that had developed among us. We set up the pup tent and managed to find enough dry wood to get a fire going. The meal lifted our spirits somewhat, but I was still uncomfortable with what I was feeling. I had felt that sense of evil and foreboding before in other places. It's common among the indigenous tribes of southwestern United States and Mexico and among Native Americans, especially near sites that have been anciently inhabited.

The rain got harder and the temperature colder, and soon we were wet, exhausted, and frozen from the thin layer of freezing rain that had built up on our jackets. The tent didn't allow three people to sleep in it at the same time, so we took shifts with two people sleeping and one keeping the fire going. We took a tin can, filled it with hot coals from the fire, and set it on a rock in the tent to take the edge off the cold.

Despite the miserable conditions, I fell asleep quickly. But soon after I'd dozed off, I was awakened by an awful commotion. My companion who was sleeping next to me had been flailing his arms wildly and had knocked the can of coals over, setting the tent on fire. I quickly got up and saw that his eyes were closed and his face looked like he was still asleep. I shook him awake, and we crawled out of the tent. We got the fire put out, but not before it had rendered the tent a lost cause. We made the best we could of the situation, but it was a terrible night.

When we awoke the next morning, the sky was still dark and the rain had only increased. It seemed like the temperature had dropped even further. The situation had become very serious and dangerous, and recognizing this helped focus our emotions a little to overcome the contention that hung in the air. We recognized that if we didn't make it up the wall and out of the canyon soon, we would be in a fatal situation.

So, with great disappointment, we looked into each other eyes and knew deep inside that there was no other recourse. We started our climb back up the canyon wall. It was obviously more difficult going up than it had been coming down, and the rain made the footing treacherous. The soil had a large quantity of clay that stuck to our feet as we tried to walk. We really hadn't gone very far when we realized that we had badly miscalculated the time required to climb up over the rocks and each one of the numerous plateaus. When possible, we would each individually find a way to get up over the rocks and on to the next level. We found many places where we had to boost each other up, and then have the one on top pull the others up to their level.

It was slow going and the little daylight passed all too rapidly. By midday, we were still less than halfway up the wall. The rain once again turned to a freezing rain, and then to a wet snow. My friend that had been argumentative the day before was on the verge of panic, and he gave voice to what we were all thinking; we had to get out of the canyon before nightfall. It would soon be night, and we would have no light at all.

We soon came to a shelf that seemed impassable. We tried everything we could think of but couldn't make it over the large overhanging rock above us. With much effort, two of us pushed the third man up the rock face until he was almost close enough to pull himself up. Just as he was about to make it, though, his foot pushed on a large rock, which dislodged from the canyon wall and fell, glancing my other friend's face. The rock was so big that it was a miracle he wasn't killed. He was hurt and bleeding, but not seriously injured. It was obvious that he had been very lucky.

When the third man's foot had slipped, he'd fallen back to the shelf we were standing on. With all three of us there, it was obvious to me that we needed some divine intervention if we were to have any hope of making it out of this canyon alive. To this end, I suggested we each individually pray out loud. Our situation had humbled us, and we each took turns petitioning our Father in Heaven for help in our difficult circumstance. The prayers were specific and sincere, and when we finished, we sat without saying a word.

After a few moments, we glanced from our shelf to the sky across the canyon, and it became very clear why it was getting increasingly darker. An absolutely pitch-black cloud was rolling in our direction from the other side of the canyon. I have never seen clouds so black. They were rolling slow, thick, and opaque, just like molasses. After our prayers, this wasn't the answer any of us had been hoping for.

As the storm front approached our side of the canyon, two large bald eagles flew out of the black morass. Majestically, the eagles flew toward us seeming to be looking directly at us then they circled back and disappeared into the black cloud.

We were speechless. Had I witnessed that alone? I don't think I could recount that story with any hopes of being believed. We sat in stunned, reverent silence, but the imminent danger represented by the change of weather soon brought us back to the moment. A tremendous snowstorm was now falling, and we couldn't see more than ten or twenty yards ahead.

After renewing our efforts to climb to the edge of the canyon, and with a more cautious selection of purchase points, we were finally able to boost the smallest man over the rock face and onto the top of the canyon. From below, we yelled for him to throw the rope, but he didn't answer. We had lost sight of him as the snowstorm grew even more intense. We tried boosting each other over the rock face, but with just the two of us, we were unsuccessful.

We were calling to our companion, screaming, but to no avail. We assumed that in his anxiety for survival he had opted to run, following his survival instincts and fleeing the storm. The two of us remaining kept trying to find a way over the ledge, but the more we tried, the more fatigued we became. Twenty or thirty minutes passed by and we still hadn't heard anything from the man that we had boosted over the top. The snowfall was so intense that the two of us could barely see each other. We leaned forward with our hands on our knees, trying to catch a breath of air.

Suddenly, with no shouting or arrival notice, a rope fell over the edge and appeared in front of our faces. Our companion had returned and thrown us a literal lifeline. We rejoiced, but even with the rope it was quite a struggle to get over the outcrop. The snow intensified, as did our efforts to liberate ourselves. This life struggle reminded me of that marathon I ran. You reach a certain point at which you just "hit a wall." Your body just says, "That's it. I'm done." From that point on, it's just a battle of mind over matter. You ask your body to do things that it reasonably doesn't want to do, and, if successful in your efforts, the battle against your body's exhaustion gets subjugated to second place. That's what happened with us on the canyon wall. The first thing on our minds, the primary battle we fought, was survival. That animal instinct to stay alive propelled us forward and allowed us to overcome the fatigue. Using all the energy we could muster, we finally made it up that rope and out of the canyon.

We were so relieved to be free from the canyon, but the next problem we faced was finding our way back to our truck and shelter. The snow was still coming down hard, and it was hard to see each other. I suggested we pray again, and the proposal was readily accepted. We all three knelt down in the middle of the blinding snow and offered up a sincere prayer.

Growing up in Utah, I had been in many snowstorms. I don't ever recall, though, having been in a snowstorm as heavy as this one. I could barely see the outline of a tree ten feet away. For safety, we took a piece of rope and tied ourselves together. Getting separated on this plateau could be a fatal mistake. One of the things we had asked in our prayer was to be able to find the truck, even though we couldn't see where we were going. As we walked, we made some course adjustments in our search according to promptings from the Spirit.

And then, all of a sudden, there it was. I can't describe the elation I felt for having found that snow-covered truck, despite how far we still had to travel over the difficult terrain. We drove for half an hour until we finally came to a place where visibility increased to twenty or thirty yards. We got out of the truck right there in the middle of the highway and changed out of our wet, cold clothes. It felt wonderful to have warm, dry clothes on again. We knew the Lord had saved us.

We eventually arrived at Hanksville and found an open restaurant. Never did a hot meal taste so good. Everything seemed so wonderful. I was seeing with a different set of eyes.

The only giants that would be of any interest to me in my future would be those that carry baseball bats. The trip, however difficult it may have been, was a powerful lesson in being humbled, in seeing how ready the Lord is to help, and in trusting how close He always is. It was an exercise that brought me to a deeper understanding of life and the consequences that result from our choices.

BUTCH AND SUNDANCE

LA PAZ, BOLIVIA

This hotel was no beauty, but at least it was vacant of bats, unlike most of the hotels in the Bolivian countryside. They had probably all left because the hotel didn't meet their cleanliness standards—or maybe it was the cold.

The cleanliness of the water was also questionable because the pipes had frozen in several places and was leaking indoors. My companions, my associate and a Bolivian guide, had wagered my breakfast against having the courage to stand in the shower long enough to wash my hair. Knowing how cheap breakfast was, I didn't think the consequences could be that bad, but when that ice cold water hit me on the head, it felt like someone had put 220 volts through me. It ended up being one of the quickest and coldest showers known to man . . . or maybe just to me.

It had been a long, rough ride from La Paz to Potosi. The roads in Bolivia are really challenging, but you can find a way when there's a financial motive. I was in the business of buying and selling gold from Bolivia at the time. The deal we had planned in Potosi appeared to have the potential to be a good business. We met with the man we planned to and then started back for La Paz. At thousands of feet above sea level, the highway was far above the timberline and the scenery was stark—and that's being generous. Still quite high in altitude, La Paz wasn't much to look at either, but arriving there after such an arduous drive was welcoming, nonetheless. Upon arriving in La Paz, we went to Chalet La Suisse, my favorite Swiss restaurant in Bolivia. The meal there was wonderful and everything seemed a lot brighter after that. A nice hot meal and a good night's rest have the potential to put even the worst of circumstances in a more tolerable condition.

Besides the ancient ruins near Lake Titicaca and the wonderful trout that came from the icy lake, La Paz didn't offer much for me. However, as I became more and more acquainted with the city over my numerous stays there over the years, I discovered some really strange things there.

For one thing, it's illegal to sell automobiles in Bolivia, because it's illegal to sell anything in Bolivia that wasn't manufactured there, and Bolivia doesn't manufacture automobiles. However, when a new model comes out in Miami, two weeks later it's on the streets of La Paz. You see the same thing with hair dryers, televisions, video games, and pretty much any other product on the market. Two days per week there is an outdoor market called *Miamicito* (Little Miami) where you can buy any product from pretty much anywhere you want. And then there's the other street market, Calle de Las Brujas, which is the street populated by witches. It's a dark place filled with an evil spirit. The witches sell all sorts of dried animal fetuses, bats, and innumerable varieties of herbs and roots.

My associate on this particular trip to Bolivia was a man in the broad-casting business whom I had previously met due to our common interest in the gold industry. One evening during out stay in La Paz, he invited me to go with him to a private club where he said excellent musicians played popular American music. He told me he would come by between eleven and eleven-thirty that night to pick me up. I told him that's the time I go home, not the time I go out. He just smiled and told me that the other side of midnight is a lot more interesting.

He picked me up on time and we went to one of the residential districts above the center of town. A valet parked his vehicle for him and we walked a couple of blocks to a dark street that had one low-wattage light sticking out from a wooden pole in a high-walled building. As we approached the light, he put his finger up to his lips for me to be quiet. I thought that was hilarious as the band inside was blasting music that could have blown the roof off. He pushed a little hard-to-see buzzer on the inside of the wall and within seconds a small window slid open in the door. A man that could have played a double for Bella Lugosi poked his face out and, apparently recognizing my companion, signaled for a young man to open the door. The young man escorted us inside to the music of Asia's "Only Time Will Tell." The music was sensational and perfectly balanced. The sound system was as fine a quality as you could find anywhere. We walked slowly through the club to see if we could locate a place to sit down. I noticed that on essentially every table there was a pile of white powder and nearly everybody had a nose and a hundred-dollar bill stuck in one of the piles.

Wayne, Bolivia.

The music was excellent, but this was not my kind of place. I told my host I was leaving, now. He told me I couldn't find any better place than this in La Paz. I told him in no uncertain terms I wanted a place where I could relax and enjoy some music for dancing, but not this. He kind of shrugged his head and said, "Okay, I know the place where everybody likes to go and have a good time and you won't see them with any white powder." My inclination was to go to bed and pull the covers over my head, but as I arrived at the new place, I noticed there was a distinctly different ambiance.

The new club, my companion told me, was where there'd be lots of beautiful happy people. As people were entering and leaving all the time, it appeared to be a decent place. We went inside and found a place to sit. Making friends was no problem. He knew everyone in the place. There was an hour or two of dancing to great music and pleasant conversation.

Then over on the far side of the club there were some angry words and a few people started pushing each other and yelling directly in other people's faces. I'm no Albert Einstein, but I recognized this as a bad omen.

As if by magic, the club split into three parts: one faction of people from Chile, one of people from Cuba, and the rest was a mix between Bolivians and Americans, each group holding their ground in a corner of the club. Everyone was glaring, cursing, and screaming in turn, almost as if the whole fight had been choreographed. My friend motioned for me to quickly move over to the side and sit down. Everything calmed down and for a moment I thought the entire situation might dissipate entirely. Knowing the potential for casualties if the fight continued, the strain and fear from the onlookers was palpable in the room, as they stiffly continued to dance, while the music innocently played on in the background.

This strained lull seemed like a good time to go, so I quickly walked up to the door. Suddenly I was surrounded by a violent group of people yelling, pushing, and pulling guns out of their jackets and the back of their pants. With my eyes as wide open as they could possibly be, I flowed outside in the middle of this mob like a stick in the Amazon River during flood season.

Almost immediately, the group split into two screaming groups. One group went to the right behind some cars and the other group to the opposite side, behind some other cars across the street. Here I was standing directly in the middle, all alone. Mouth open, eyes open, and all the adrenaline of a gazelle flowing through my veins. I was posed to set a new land speed record to the nearest point of safety. With the yelling escalating, all guns seemed to be pointed at me in a cross fire. My head spun almost completely around as I surveyed my right and left flanks for even the tiniest shelter to crawl under. Both groups were screaming, waving their guns and threatening to fire, each baiting the other one to make the first move. Then, this American whiz kid realized that when one of them fired, they would all fire. This situation had apparently been brewing for a long time in the club, and now on the street, the reality was they wanted to shoot each other, and I was right in the middle of them. There was a pickup truck parked against the curb, and I figured that was my best hope. With an Olympic sprinter's gold-medal bolt, I ran so fast that I felt my cheeks flapping in the wind. I leaped in the air in a perfect swan dive into the back of a truck. I banged my knee on the top of the bed. It really hurt later, but at this stage of the game, the adrenaline masked any pain. I expected my whole body to be full of bullet holes at any moment. I lay there squinting, wondering which bullets would come first—the Chileans' or the Cubans.'

As the shouting and threats continued, the man that brought me to this lovely little cultural exchange ran up, crouching down, and yelled at me to get out of the truck and follow him NOW. I looked around and, not seeing any danger in his direction, ran after him. By the time I got to his car, the seats were already full of people, in shock and pale with fear. Somebody opened the hatchback window. I dove right into the back of the car, and we drove away, kicking up rocks in our escape. Like in some b-grade apocalyptic horror film, gangs of people started chasing us. I had no clue as to who or why—I just wanted to get out of there as fast as I could. Like in a Jurassic Park scene where the T-rex was chasing the Jeep, we were all saying and thinking, "We must go faster, we must go faster." These were small city blocks in the center of La Paz and by the time we'd get to one corner, the gang had arrived at the next corner.

After some rounds of cat and mouse, we finally got around them and were able to leave that part of the city. The experiences in Bolivia taught me a lot of good lessons and left me with a strong urge to watch *Butch Cassidy and the Sundance Kid*.

STREET FIGHT IN KOREA

IRI, KOREA

M r. Lee, my representative in Iri, Korea,[1] went to collect a debt another company owed me. He went because he was my agent in Korea and was therefore responsible for all my shipments and payments there. The man who owed the debt was very argumentative and refused to pay the bill. He then made a sad mistake: he tried to hit Mr. Lee, who, though a short man, was a very highly trained martial arts expert and swiftly broke the other man's nose and jaw. When the fighting began, all the workers from both factories ran into the street and a huge martial arts battle ensued. And who was the fall guy in the middle of it all? My representative, Mr. Lee.

After that outbreak, the workers left the factory angry with Mr. Lee and his supervisors for starting the fight. They went on strike on the grounds that the supervisors were hitting them too much, which was a regular occurrence and normal consequence for mistakes made in the Korean culture. Despite their strike there was still a debt to be paid so I made the trip out to Korea to handle the situation, hoping to have the matter dealt with in a few days.

The next day, the workers returned and one by one came back to ask for forgiveness for the time they had missed in producing the cubic zirconia. They agreed to work for free until all the missed time was made up. When they asked forgiveness they were on the floor, balanced on their foreheads and toes. That was one of the most astonishing acts of self-discipline and strength I had ever seen. You have to be in very good shape to be able to get on your forehead and toes, let alone to stay in that position for several minutes with your hands behind your back. Talk about asking for forgiveness! I was astonished and thought it barbaric for them to have to ask for forgiveness in this manner.

I began to loudly convey my disapproval to Mr. Lee, his factory manager, and the supervisor who normally took employee issues to management. Mr. Lee explained to me that I was from a different world and didn't understand their customs. *Yeah, no kidding*, I thought. He said the apparent punishment was really a form of self-discipline and recommitment, proving their allegiance to the company. Nobody disliked the company; on the contrary, they loved the company and were willing to sacrifice whatever it took to help it be successful.

These Korean people were amazing. I didn't understand their culture—many experiences taught me that.

A few days later, Mr. Lee asked me if I was interested in learning the Korean language. I just laughed and told him it would probably take a long time. He agreed and said he thought it would take at least until the weekend. He had to be joking. But once I realized Mr. Lee was very serious about teaching me, I agreed to learn.

He said the martial arts he studied was very much like their language. He started by showing me some of their basic martial art stances. Each was accompanied by a distinctive sound, which sounded like a series of grunting noises to me. As he repeated them, though, they began to sound more natural. He would say them in a loud, martial arts–type manner, making the corresponding sign by arranging his body and limbs in different positions.

Well, we practiced the sounds with their matching body positions, and by the second day, I could see a word in Korean and repeat it. I began showing off a little bit and left a lot of people absolutely flabbergasted, including myself. Now I didn't really know any vocabulary, but I could see a sign and read what it said in Korean. This was really amazing. All I had to do now was work on improving my vocabulary. I never quite mastered Korean, but I learned that it is a beautiful and elegant language, albeit very different from English.

Another experience that showed me how different Korean and American cultures are was when I went to a restaurant there. When you are in Korea or Hong Kong or Bangkok, it's expected and mandatory that whoever your representative is (or whoever is negotiating with and trying to do business with you) always takes you out for lunch and dinner. Before

I went to Korea, a number of people had told me how terrible the food was, and I nearly gagged as they described *kimchi*, a fermented cabbage that has a very strong odor and is quite spicy. When Mr. Lee invited me to go eat with him, I wasn't at all excited to eat traditional Korean food. But I didn't want to insult my host, so I tried to act as excited as I could.

The restaurant we went to was one of the most amazing and disgusting things I have ever seen. It was an eel restaurant with dozens of large fish tanks full of two- or three-foot eels. I had had a lot of experience with snakes, but these were horrible-looking creatures that looked particularly slimy. Eels were the main dish of the restaurant and were accompanied by small dishes of bean paste and green peppers. I didn't want to hurt Mr. Lee's feelings, but I told him that though I could probably handle the vegetable dishes, eating eels was just too much to ask. He politely smiled and said that was okay.

As we ate I discovered that the little side dishes were really quite good, but every time I looked at one of those eel tanks I just about lost my meal. After a few minutes, the waiter brought an eel, cooked barbecue style. Against my better judgment, I had to admit that the eel looked and smelled good. I ventured a bite, and made a surprising discovery: barbecued eel was one of the most flavorful dishes I had ever eaten! The accompanying dishes were also fabulous, once I learned how to combine

Piles of mined rose quartz and purple quartz, which Wayne discovered. Shipments such as these were sent to Hong Kong and Korea.

them. The longer I stayed in Korea, the better the food seemed, and the more I appreciated their culture.

While there I learned a lot about Korea, its food, and customs, and I really began to love it, aside from the problems I had with my business shipment of twenty tons of rose quartz and crystal. The paperwork for the shipment was all messed up, and because it was only a week or two before Christmas I didn't know if I would have time to fix it. And I certainly didn't want to be on the other side of the world from my family over Christmas. But the negotiations got more difficult by the day, and it was starting to look like I would have to stay there over the holidays or risk losing a large sum of money—at least seventy or eighty thousand dollars, possibly more.

Time continued to pass and I became more discouraged each day. Before I knew it, it was Christmas Eve. I hadn't managed to fix the problems, I hadn't made it home for Christmas, and I was really down and out. I decided to go for a walk and see if I could cheer up a little bit.

I left the hotel and ended up by an outdoor market with many different products for sale. I saw some little pet dogs they had for sale. They looked like they would be the perfect present for my kids. As I neared the market, however, I was traumatized: a man behind the counter grabbed one of the animals, hit it on the head and tossed it into a large pot of boiling water with some vegetables mixed in. After about a minute the man took the dog out of the pot, pulled its hair off and started cutting it into pieces with a heavy, sharp knife. Here I had gone for a soothing walk to reflect on the meaning of Christmas and I had run into a scene that I was totally unprepared for. I was fighting a losing battle with nausea, and I knew that if I didn't leave soon I might add my half-digested breakfast to the man's pot. So I headed back to the hotel to escape the traumatic scene and get out of the snow.

I walked slowly down the street, discouraged about being away from home and having no basis whatsoever for the cultural customs in Korea. And then, walking toward me, were two Mormon missionaries, name tags and all. We exchanged greetings, visited for a while, and then with well wishes and pats on the back, we went our separate ways, my spirits lifted.

I was grateful that day for a Father in Heaven who was watching out for me and knew what I needed to cheer up. Since that experience, I have had many more that have solidified this principle in my mind: God knows and loves us, and He watches out for us wherever we are in the world.

NOTES

1.   Iri, Korea, is now Iksa, Korea.

UP THE CREEK WITHOUT A PADDLE

MEXICO

I don't know why my buddies and I decided this was an adventure worth taking. The place had been described to us as full of ancient artifacts from the Mayan and other contemporary cultures. I guess that's what really caught our interest. But it was far way—it was numerous days of nonstop driving. There were four of us, and we took turns driving, riding shotgun, and sleeping. It was quite the setup for a group of college kids.

One of my companions, Stan Johnson, had made this journey once before. He not only provided us with the transportation—the Volkswagen bus and the canoe—but he served as our guide as well. He was by far the greatest resource on this adventure.

The area we were going to was in southern Mexico. The deeper we went into Mexico, the more excited we became. Along the way we visited museums, archaeological zones, pyramids, and many other structures typical of ancient cultures. Our ultimate plan for this trip was to go up the Coatzacoalcos River to explore some caves that one of the members of our group had previously been to. When we arrived at the city Jesús Carranza, everyone got excited because it was close to the area where we would launch our boat. As I look back on it now, I am embarrassed at how amateurish we must have looked, but hey, when you're having the time of your life, who cares?

We pulled up near a humble little home on the edge of the river and explained to the residents that we were going on a trip upriver for several days and asked permission to leave our van under their care. They were very kind and generous and seemed to be getting a big kick out of all our gear, including our fiberglass canoe with its Johnson 10 hp motor. The natives looked over our equipment and cameras, and as they did, I could imagine them saying, "Umm. Plenty good, Great White Treasure Hunter from the Northland."

After looking at our canoe, they proudly showed us their canoes. They were wooden dugout canoes that had been handmade and looked pretty rustic. Although we didn't understand everything that was said, it was easy to see that each man took pride in the craftsmanship of his wooden canoe.

It was late in the afternoon and we wanted to get as much distance behind us as we could before nightfall, so we took our fiberglass canoe, put it in the water, and mounted the motor. We had sleeping bags, cameras, and backpacks containing miscellaneous food and equipment. Quite a few of the natives had gathered around to watch this great spectacle. Because we had so much weight in the canoe, we had to be very careful getting on board. When all four of us were finally in the canoe with all our gear, we had about two inches of freeboard. That meant that if anybody made any sudden movements (like sneezing) we would probably sink.

At the sight of this situation, the Indians couldn't contain themselves anymore. They were laughing hysterically at this parade of clowns. We knew we wouldn't get far this way, so very gingerly, and with the help of their ropes, we got our canoe back to shore without drowning. They suggested that we rent a dugout canoe from them, put one man and most of our gear in it and pull him behind our canoe with a strong cord. We didn't have much of a choice. We rented the canoe, knowing that this wasn't exactly our best National Geographic moment. I'm sure it's one the Indians will remember for a long time to come though.

But the moment that really topped it all off was when the owner of the house asked if he could take a picture of us with his camera. It really was hilarious. We were beyond embarrassment by this point, so we obliged, joining in on the laughter.

We started off slowly and did pretty well, all things considered. The river is a pretty good size and can be very treacherous when there are rain showers upstream. We only had three oars between the two canoes, but that seemed to be okay.

As we went upriver, I was enchanted with the beauty of the jungle, but the pyramids were what really fascinated me. I can't say exactly how many, but there were a large number of pyramids, largely covered in vegetation, along the riverbank. The whole place was very overgrown, but despite this I could still see very clearly that there were many pyramids, temples, and other similar buildings in the area. I was really amazed at how much ancient architecture was still untouched in the jungles of Central and South America. During a discussion with a very prominent Mexican archaeologist in Mexico City, we had learned that an estimated 80 percent of the structures of ancient America have never been excavated. All the structures we saw confirmed what I have always felt—that there are many great and wonderful discoveries still waiting to come forth. Along with this feeling came one of apprehension: I was so excited about seeing all these undiscovered and unexcavated ancient cities that I knew if I ever got started it would be hard to leave. I tried to keep a notebook of what we were seeing, but the river became more treacherous and we soon had to devote all our attention to navigating.

By this time it was starting to get late, and we knew it was best to pick a good spot while we still had enough light to see. We found some pretty wide sandbars that looked like they would do just fine and set up camp. We were still very excited about this new adventure, with all the wild animals, strange and exotic natives, countless ancient structures, and so many stories waiting to be told.

The next morning I woke up totally alert and excited to get on with the day's prospects. We planned to have a good breakfast in preparation for the challenges of the day. But when we went back to the dugout to look for food, we found, to our dismay and aggravation, a giant cylindrical box of oatmeal unsealed among the packs. Every camera, every rope, every piece of clothing was completely coated with a half-inch layer of old-fashioned oats. I'm still not sure how it happened, but it made for a revolting situation. So there we were, at the site of our archaeological dreams and the sum of all our adventures, and we were cleaning copious amounts of oatmeal off all our belongings. Since then, I have never looked at oatmeal the same way.

We were all pretty grumpy but we managed to get everything cleaned up as best as we could. Before we left, we had a nice prayer kneeling down on a sandbar. After that, everyone seemed to feel much better. I am sure we needed that prayer more than we knew. Because of the darkness the night before and our excitement about being there, we hadn't realized that this really was a challenging area. The river surrounding us could rise or fall as much as twenty feet in a matter of minutes as a result of the heavy rains upstream.

We hooked the boats back up again, and took off to conquer the world. That was a long day. Close to dark we drew near the area we were looking for. The village we were going to was only a quarter of a mile away, but there was a formidable obstacle between the village and us: a swamp. It was a slimy, muddy, nasty bog, but we had traveled thousands of miles and weren't about to stop because of a bit of mud. After walking a short distance in the swamp, however, it became evident that this would be a very difficult place to traverse. We went back to our campsite to talk about what we should do. As we were sitting, contemplating what we should do, several children wandered into the campsite. We looked at them, and when they saw us they ran away in the direction of the swamp as if they had just seen Godzilla. We were deep in the jungle, and these children had probably never seen people that looked like us before. We could hear them off in the distance with a mixture of frightened yells and amazed discovery. The thought of plodding through the mud after them wasn't very attractive, so we decided to just sit down and wait them out.

After about fifteen minutes they showed up again, this time with three or four young men who looked like they were between the ages of eighteen and twenty. Despite their age, however, the older boys were really very similar to the little boys. They were all very shy and cautious, but one of the members of our group spoke excellent Spanish and won them over in a very short while. When we asked about the swamp, they said we would have to go by boat or canoe and be very careful, as there were a lot of snakes in the swamp, many of which were very dangerous. They told us that the two most poisonous snakes were what they called the "five stepper" and the "ten stepper." We learned that these snakes were aptly named—after being bitten by one, you walked either five or ten steps before you died.

After giving that harrowing definition, they really didn't have to tell us to be cautious as we crossed the swamp. We started making our way across it, and everyone was on guard with a sharp machete. We hadn't gone ten feet into the swamp before snakes started slithering through the swamp in every direction. Growing up in the mountains of Utah, I had had quite a bit of experience with snakes, especially water snakes and blow snakes. In our younger days, we used to go to the carnival that came to Heber City every year, put the snakes inside our shirts, and then open our shirts to the girls. It was pretty easy to get a reaction and we always got a big kick out of it, but I think it's safe to say the girls didn't appreciate it very much. But those snakes couldn't compare with the size of the snakes in that swamp. Needless to say, I wasn't about to put one of those down my shirt.

We moved slowly through the swamp of snakes. I thought about the plague of snakes the Lord had cursed the unrighteous people with in the Book of Mormon. Thinking about those "fiery flying serpents" (1 Nephi 17:41) put me on edge even more, and after that, I constantly and intently searched the water and the banks for snakes.

But I didn't think to look up for the snakes. A large brown one about as big around as my arm fell out of a tree and brushed my shoulder before hitting the water with a noise that sounded like a cannon going off. It all happened so fast I about fell out of the canoe. After that encounter, my machete was constantly poised for action.

We saw the strangest creatures as we plowed our way through the swamp. I saw a lizard that was about a foot long, and its four legs pumped so fast it could walk on water. A footlong lizard wouldn't normally frighten anyone, but when you've never seen one like it before and it's coming straight at you, you want to run on the water too, except in the other direction. We each had our share of discoveries, adventures, and frights in the swamp. When we finally set foot in the village, it was like we were being welcomed to Times Square.

The people were dressed a lot like we imagined their ancestors would have dressed centuries earlier. Everyone was outfitted in simple light-weight clothing. Everything about this village was exactly as we had imagined it would be.

It was starting to get dark by the time we arrived, and we were all hungry. One of the natives suggested we come with him and catch our dinner. I wasn't so sure this was such a bright idea (I certainly didn't want to catch a five stepper or the lizard that could walk on water), but I wanted to make a good impression on the natives. I followed him and the rest of my group to a stream of clear water that ran along the edge of the vil-lage. Our guide told us that when we saw two green lights shining in the water we were to reach down and grab it. I wanted to know what "it" was before I grabbed it. He said "it" was nothing harmful—just shrimp. That sounded pretty good, but I still wasn't totally convinced.

We hadn't waded far before we saw dozens of green eyes staring back at us. I thought they would have to be the biggest shrimp I had ever seen, based on how spread apart their eyes were. Our guide took the first one for us. The footlong shrimp looked a lot less threatening when held in somebody's hand than it did when its two green eyes shone at us from the dark water. The shrimp squirmed a little but the guide would just roll them into the bottom portion of his T-shirt. After watching him, we overcame our fear and started catching them alongside our guide. In no time at all we were on our way to the kitchen with plenty of delicious-looking shrimp.

We hadn't gone far when we met a group of men coming from the village, two of them were holding a large tray with a boar's head on it. They had just killed the wild boar, and as we were their honored guests they wanted to save the best part for us. I thought to myself, *Oh yummy. Isn't that just delicious?* Eating shrimp was one thing; eating the head of a wild boar was quite another.

The line from the Lone Ranger came to me, "That plenty bad, kemos-abe." I wasn't excited about the prospect of eating the boar's head, but I also didn't want to offend any of our new friends, who might get just as much delight from seeing a gringo on one of those platters as from seeing a wild boar. It was ugly as sin, and we were all trying to think of a way to avoid eating it, but we agreed that if we didn't just smile and eat it, we might offend them. They started cutting off some slices from the "really good part"—the nose. They took the slices and wrapped them in a tortilla. I wasn't really sure I'd be able to stomach it, but I had heard too many stories of gringos offending their hosts and getting a "Mexican suntan." So I just closed my eyes, breathed a silent prayer, and took a bite. Then I made the strangest discovery of all: it was good! It tasted sort of like roast pork. What an amazing and delicious surprise. My testimony of the power of prayer had been strengthened, and I knew that the Lord had saved my bacon, pardon my pun, once again.

We spent several days in the village, and we didn't make any of the great discoveries we had hoped to make, but we made a few other discoveries. What I didn't realize until sometime later was that the trip and the experiences we had were the real treasures. Yes, we went into giant caves with millions of bats, and yes, we dug for ancient buried treasure, but the real adventure and the real challenges had yet to come. We eventually said goodbye to our new friends and left the village. Part of that friendship was possible because two members of our group were professional artists and really got the natives excited when they drew portraits of them. They took it as a great honor and treated us very well.

Oh, there was one more thing I forgot to mention . . .

On the first night of our stay, I set up my little pup tent on the top of a small knoll overlooking the swamp. We were all very tired and went to sleep quickly. Sometime in the middle of the night, I felt something touch my lower back. I was lying on my right side up against the side of the nylon tent. I could feel whatever it was slithering along the outside of my cheap tent and up my back. Whatever it was, it was very long and scaly. Was I providing comforting warmth to a large snake? Was it a ten stepper? A five stepper? Either one meant certain death—the difference was a mere five steps. To really understand the implications of the word slithering you have to experience it. And once is enough—that will give you all of the understanding you'll ever need on that subject.

As I lay there, I didn't know what to do. My little pup tent offered no real protection from the snake at all. I was afraid to holler or jump or try to unzip the tent and get out. Ironically, it was probably that fear, as much as anything else, that made me stay still. I was sweating and hot, but the hotter I became, the more Mr. Ten Stepper would nuzzle in closer. I lay there praying as I had never prayed before, and after what seemed to be an eternity my new friend slithered away. What a night that was.

The morning we decided to leave, our new friends led the way. We were escorted out of the swamp without any real problems, other than seeing several hundred snakes. But after sharing a tent with an alleged ten stepper, how bad could a few snakes be?

We got down on the sandbar at the edge of the river, and most of the village had somehow managed to make their way through the swamp to see us off. It was cloudy and apparently there had been heavy rains upstream. Because the current was moving fast and the waves were getting bigger and bigger, we lashed all our equipment down tightly and tied a strong rope between the two canoes. We had three paddles between the four of us, and one man on the motor. That gave us all some degree of steering and made it possible to navigate through the treacherous parts of the stream. This was quite different from the slow pace we had used on our way there. When we came upstream, we went as slow as the boat would allow. Going downstream, however, there was no choice but to move rapidly. Before long we were going faster than we had ever anticipated.

The rains upstream must have been quite severe, because the river was rising dramatically and the current was increasing in speed. We joked about this at first, but the laughter was short-lived.

We wanted to get out of the current and find some shelter and safety, but the water was so fierce it kept breaking down the banks on both sides of the river and didn't leave us any place to go ashore. It was absolutely amazing how fast the rain had driven the water up. We were not adequately prepared and were on the verge of paying very dearly for it. We struggled with the oars to keep our boats moving between the rocks so they wouldn't get crushed or tipped over. But no matter how big the rocks we passed were, every few minutes we encountered bigger ones.

Suddenly, we saw a really amazing and welcoming sight: a large wooden dugout canoe coming downstream. There were about twenty Mexican men in the canoe and they saw us just in time to get a line over to us. The swiftness of the water swung the three canoes (now tied together) in a big arc that carried us through the rapids and over to a newly formed bank. The fiberglass canoe hit the bank hard, but the big dugout canoe had enough stability and weight to keep us from tipping over (the rescuers in the long dugout canoe worked for an oil company and had tied the boats together very well). After that, we pulled the rented wooden dugout up to put it close to our fiberglass canoe and started off downstream with a lot more stability than our little canoe had had by itself.

After an hour or two, the rain began to subside and the world started to look a little friendlier. It wasn't until then that we realized the evident excitement of our new friends. They told us that they had been doing some drilling upstream and had found a major oil reserve. That reserve turned out to be one of the biggest in Mexican history and really gave their economy a boost starting in the latter half of the 1970s. When they spotted us, they were on their way to announce their great petroleum discovery to the world. I am very glad they didn't make their discovery any later, or we would have ended up at the bottom of the river!

This turned out to really be an amazing trip and one that none of us will ever forget. To this day, whenever I see the Petromex logo I think of snakes, hidden caves, and large oil reserves—all the elements of a great adventure.

CELESTIAL COMPANION

SÃO PAULO, BRAZIL

São Paulo is one of the largest cities in the world. I had traveled extensively for many years, but I was still a country boy from Heber City, Utah. Trying to absorb the enormous structure and function of a city as big as São Paulo was really a challenge. I hired a taxi driver to take me around and show me some safe areas I could potentially live in. I had been offered a proposal to move to São Paulo and start a satellite communications company for some men. One of the homes I visited in the first few days I really liked but had turned down because of cost. I was growing tired of living in a hotel after a couple months and decided to go back to this particular house. I had a feeling I should speak again with the owner. It was a very nice home and highly unlikely it would still be available after all this time. But I had a feeling about it that I needed to pursue.

I had the real estate agent go with me to the house. As before, the lady who owned the house invited us in and told us to make ourselves at home. This was one thing that had caught my interest during the first visit. She was nice, friendly, and courteous and I believed that this house was meant for me. She said several people had looked at the house and wanted to rent it, but she said she knew I was coming back and she was saving the house for me. I was stunned. I couldn't deny the impression that we had apparently both received. We concluded the deal.

I was quite satisfied with the outcome. But it was more than just the satisfaction of finding a nice and safe place to live. I didn't know what it was at the time, but I did know that God was involved in my living there.

When I had lived in Florida, Brazilians would often come to church and the bishop would usually funnel them directly to me because I was fluent in Portuguese. Over a period of time, I had met and become friends with many Brazilians. Spending time with them was always an enjoyable experience. They have a happy disposition and love to laugh.

Well now that I was living back in Brazil, I found out where the nearest LDS chapel was and went there on Sunday morning. Everybody treated me just wonderfully. The members' kindness helped confirm the feeling that I had needed to return to Brazil. I sat down on one of the benches and looked around a little bit to see the people I was likely to have a lot of contact with in the future. I hadn't been sitting for more than a minute when a sister behind me tapped me on the shoulder and said, "Hey, I know you. I know you from Orlando. You're the one that took us to the temple." At first, I didn't recognize her, as there had been many visitors over the years from Brazil. She then introduced me to her children. Funny, I hadn't recognized the mother but I had recognized one of the daughters who was fifteen or sixteen. She said she had a silkscreened T-shirt at home that had a photo of her family and me at the Orlando Temple. As I looked at the little family, I began to remember. It was just a joy to imagine that somebody who had lived so far away from me could remember who I was. The mother invited me over for dinner after church. The church meetings were wonderful, the food the family gave me at was fabulous and their home was really amazing in every aspect, especially size. I got many more invites from ward members for dinner over the next few weeks and each was delightful. I was really enjoying myself and making many new friends.

However, I was growing slightly annoyed that so many people, especially the bishop, continued to ask where my wife was.[1] I explained that I hadn't been married for about eleven years and didn't have any desire to have a wife now. When Bishop Paulo heard this, he was simply beside himself. He said, "How do you expect the Lord to bless you if you don't have a wife and aren't looking for one? You have to have a celestial companion to close the celestial route. You've got to pray. You've got to pray every day. If you don't pray the Lord just can't help you. Where's your faith? Think about all the spiritual blessings you'll miss if you don't have an eternal marriage." I wasn't used to being pushed so hard and felt some chafing and told him so, but it didn't make one iota of difference. He said I had to pray and get a wife and I had to do it soon.

I just told him to slow down a little and give me some room, and he did, for a whole week. The next Sunday, as I was leaving the church, the bishop brought me over lovingly by the arm and making introductions, said, "This is sister Nilva Nardi and her son Fellipe and they were just baptized today."

I don't know how to adequately explain what happened next because the sensation was unfamiliar, but there was such warmth, such radiance, such a sense of anticipation, I was really jolted. I had never seen such a beautiful smile, radiating optimism and energy. She had such a friendly nature about her. I lost my composure a little and tried not to appear as the blithering idiot I felt like at that moment. The bishop asked me on the way out if I had been doing as he asked, meaning praying for a wife of course. I was about to tell him no and to stop bugging me, but at that instant I realized that I had said a prayer or two during the week. A wife hadn't appeared at my doorway at the end of the prayer, so I figured that was as good an answer as I needed. However, I hadn't anticipated meeting anyone later and having such feelings in my heart. I don't know if anyone there recognized the love struck symptoms I was experiencing, but if they had, they would have had a good laugh on my behalf.

It seemed like everyone at church was doing the best Cupid work they could. There were parties, dances, and activities—none of them ever seemed to end. Nilva and I were both always on the guest lists. There was no doubt that I had feelings for her and we always seemed to be thrown together, so I'm not sure why I hesitated to ask her out. Maybe it was because I had some battle scars that still prompted me to be cautious. One of the ladies I knew from church called and said she and Nilva wanted to go out to dinner but thought that it would be improper in Brazilian society for them to go unescorted. She asked if I would do the great favor of helping them out by going out to dinner with them. And she said not to worry; they would pay for their own dinners. I've seen a lot of ambushes, but this one was blatant. I escorted them to dinner and we all had a wonderful evening, yet I still didn't make a move.

One Sunday, Nilva confronted me about a play she had invited me to. She had never heard a response and wanted to know why I didn't at least call her back. I told her I had never received the message or I certainly would have called her back. Unfortunately, I had been really busy doing a lot of traveling. I said, "How would you like to go to a movie at the shopping center tomorrow evening? And this time I'll pay the bill." That brought a big laugh and she agreed. We decided we would meet at the theater box office. I got there ahead of time and noticed her when she was still quite a ways down the hallway. She had on black knee-length boots, a white skirt and a purple sweater. She had a sparkle in her eye, a beautiful smile, and looked like she owned the world. What a sight. I had never felt my heart race like that before.

Cinemas are very popular in Brazil—beautiful, with excellent popcorn. There were hundreds of people waiting to get tickets. We walked together over to the side of the crowd near the front. A man walked up to us and said he had two free tickets to get into the theater and offered them to us. If I had been looking for a sign I surely had it.

During the eleven years since that night we have spent very few nights apart. I am grateful that despite how confident I was to be without a wife, the Lord saw a different plan for me. Most Brazilians are given a hard lot in life and merely survive the circumstances of each day. But not Nilva. She overcame her challenges.

NOTES

1.   I was currently unmarried, although I had been married twice before. My first wife had passed away and I was divorced from my second wife.

NILVA'S STORY

SÃO PAULO, BRAZIL

C ome on, it's time to get up. You've got a lot of work to do," her mother said, as she entered the room.

"Could I stay in just one day? It's so cold." Nilva was shaking from the cold but she knew she would be shaking much harder if she disobeyed her mother.

The routine was always the same. Get up early, go to school, and then hurry back, put on her rubber boots and go to the trash pile to dig for cans which were sold and the funds used for food for her mother, her sister, and herself. She had to be very careful where she went to pick up her cans. There were guards that carried shovels that were used to beat the children that tried to get cans for themselves. She felt very angry within herself at the situation, but at the same time was grateful that at least they had this to keep them alive.

Nilva thought about many things during her morning and afternoon walks to and from the trash pile. Her rubber boots were very uncomfortable and hurt her feet to walk. The socks, even though they were ragged and torn, helped take up some of the space in the boots and made it a little more comfortable, but her feet were still very cold.

Sometimes she allowed her thoughts to wander to dream of Prince Charming, big tables of delicious hot food, beautiful dresses, and a mansion with a swimming pool and servants. She knew they weren't real and never would be, but they brought many pleasant moments as she struggled to pry the cans away from the giant behemoth that held them captive.

Occasionally she allowed her thoughts to reflect back on the peaceful times she had enjoyed with her father, before he had left. She missed him and didn't get to see him often, even though he only lived a relatively short distance away. She remembered the times she would sit on his lap with her head on his chest and he would tell her stories.

———

The day he left was filled with anticipation for her birthday. She was really anxious for the birthday cake and even though she would be the one to make it, it would be *her* cake for *her* birthday. She knew her piece wouldn't be very big because it would have to be shared with the neighbors that would be there to join in the celebration, but it would be her birthday cake nonetheless.

Her mother said she couldn't promise, but there was a possibility of a new dress. She knew from experience not to expect too much. Things rarely turned out the way she wanted them to. Nevertheless, she let dreams of happiness fill her thoughts.

Her pleasant thoughts were interrupted by a commotion started by rapid talking from her parent's bedroom and increased until both of them were screaming at each other.

"Oh please, not now," Nilva pleaded to herself.

Yet the shouting continued and was followed by loud banging as chairs, pictures, and other things in the bedroom crashed against the wall and then dropped to the floor.

She was sure her father's anger was because her mother had given his books away. The final insult to her father had been that she had not even asked for anything for the books, not even for a few meager *cruzeiros*. They always fought and argued and she didn't like that. It scared her.

Her mother had sold her father's most precious possession, his books, over eight hundred of them, especially those on politics and government, and given them to a second-hand bookshop, which rapidly dispersed them throughout the city. His prized possessions had been irretrievably lost.

Her father appeared in the bedroom door with one large and two small suitcases in hand. He glanced briefly at Nilva with a look of despair on his face. He turned and walked out the door without uttering a word. Just like that he was gone.

Her parents had fought frequently during the last several months, but never like this. She knew in her heart he wouldn't be coming back. Pain and anxiety shot through her chest like a bolt of lightning. She ran to the door after her father, but to no avail. He didn't even acknowledge her cries of despair. Her mother ran up beside her and struck her on the side of the head with such force it sent her tumbling. Her father didn't even look.

Quite a few of the neighbors just stood around looking and waiting to see if anything more might happen. Nothing did, and they gradually wandered away. Nilva was sitting on the veranda when her mother walked by and dropped a crumpled off-white dress on her lap without saying a word.

Nilva fought the urge to look at the dress. She sat for some time, quiet, trying to find some basis of comprehension for the day's events. She stroked the dress softly, sensing the texture, finally looking at it. The dress was beautiful, but a small recompense for losing her father. Even hurting as she was, she couldn't resist the excitement she felt in her stomach at the beauty of the dress. It was a very light cream color with heavier than normal cotton material covered with embroidered flower designs. She resisted the desire to put it on until Wanda, one of her friends who lived nearby, walked up to admire the dress.

Nilva put it on and was amazed at how good it made her feel. She said a silent prayer of thanks, and told God she would always take care of it. She felt much better and easily agreed to make a cake at Wanda's urging.

Both Nilva and Wanda thought it would be much better to stay out of the kitchen and Nilva's mother's way. Nilva got her play stove and some alcohol and they went down the swale a short distance so as to not disturb Nilva's mother. Nilva held a metal cup and Wanda filled it with alcohol. They would ignite the fuel, put the cup in the oven and let it warm up while they mixed the batter. Wanda struck a match and the fuel popped to life. Nilva started to set the oven down, but some of the alcohol had splashed on her fingers and it began to burn. She called out in distress and Wanda grabbed the alcohol-filled cup and threw it in the air.

The alcohol, rather than going to the side she had intended, splashed on Nilva's head and chest. Nilva shrieked in pain as she turned into an instant ball of fire. Immediately, Wanda grabbed a bucket of water and dowsed Nilva to put out the flames. Unbeknownst to Wanda, the bucket was filled with alcohol, not water.

The giant ball of flames that was Nilva grew larger, encompassing her whole body. A neighbor ran from his house and threw a blanket around her to extinguish the flames, but instead of dowsing the fire, the flames shot upward, burning her face and the hair on the back of her head. Her hair sizzled as it turned into carbon. The burning of her eyelashes and eyebrows caused pain beyond comprehension as they disintegrated. She was in total panic, and amazing as it was that she had any rationale remaining, she headed for the well. The skin on her whole body was burning and she tried to brush the burning hair off her head, but that made it hurt worse. Large patches of skin came off with what was left of her hair.

Another neighbor, seeing the situation, ran as fast as he could and threw a bucket of water on her just before she got to the well. The flames were dowsed and cold liquid dripped off her scorched body.

By now her mother had arrived and she tried to pick her up, but all the skin on her legs came off. This woman who had been so harsh and unrelenting and who herself had been hardened as the granddaughter of a slave, held her poor, suffering child in her arms and wept uncontrollably. However, there was another nightmarish challenge in front of them. The only transportation was a bicycle. It had a carrying rack and they outfitted it the best they could with pillows, starting off for the hospital, which was over an hour away.

The doctor was heartbroken when he saw Nilva. He groaned sympathetically as he started removing the plastic looking skin, flaking off in large pieces. He took his tweezers and started pulling in the navel. The skin in the navel came out in nearly one piece. Nilva whimpered in pain.

At long last, when the burnt skin was removed and her body was covered with an antibiotic salve, she was covered with white bandages and instructed to return every day for a week to repeat the treatment. After that she could get the treatment done at her neighborhood pharmacy. Then came something that Nilva would regard as the most painful part of the whole experience. He gave her a penicillin injection along with something he called crystals. When the injection was in the system the horrendous pain was beyond anything she had ever experienced. At times the burning was so intense she fainted from the pain.

It took many months for her to recover, and a year or two for the miracle to take place. The miracle was and is that she completely recovered and doesn't have any noticeable scars when it was assumed by all that she would go through life horribly disfigured. God's greatest miracles are frequently brought to pass by those who know severe suffering and can relate to the humble and lowly in heart.

Another miraculous event that took place during that dark and challenging day was that when they examined Nilva's dress, they could not find one thread that had so much as been singed. Nilva always thought it was because she had been so grateful for it and had promised God she would take care of it.

Nilva's father didn't come back for a long time, and when he did, the visits were infrequent and short. Every time he visited, he and her mother had a bad argument about something. When Nilva went to his house where he lived with his new wife, she wasn't treated very well and it always made her feel terrible to make the long walk back home by herself, especially because it was a dangerous area.

But while life was hard for Nilva, there were a few people that showed kindness and offered her help. Sometimes it wasn't very much help, but it was all appreciated. There was a fishmonger who came with a horse-drawn wagon once a week. When Nilva would run along beside him, he frequently would throw her a couple of fish. That was a wonderful treat and brought Nilva a lot of praise because she did all the cooking. Her mother and her sister didn't do any cooking. From the time she was seven years old, with the exception of the many months she was healing from the burn, Nilva came home from school, put her boots on and went to the garbage pile to pull out metal cans which she used for buying food for her family. She then took the food home and prepared a meal. She was responsible for all the cooking and cleaning at home, similar to Cinderella. Nilva was forced to do all the work because of the darkness of her complexion. Her sister had a fair complexion, which was admired and meant that the work fell upon the dark one.

Nilva got to be a very good cook and gained a certain amount of fame in the area where she lived. She was especially famous for her cakes, which often had a cream filling and frosting on the outside. Not bad for a seven-year-old.

During one of Nilva's daily walks, she thought about the old black and white TV set that had been sitting in her mother's bedroom for some time. It looked like an old-fashioned radio with a small twelve-inch screen in the middle. Her father had brought it home, but it had never worked.

Nilva had a good idea. She took it to a repairman and made a deal to pay off the repairs within three weeks. It took about a week to get the repair parts in and based on her good name in the community, he let her take it home.

To say the neighborhood was excited was putting it mildly. They were in an anticipated frenzy. They would get to see Jornal Nacional, Globo's opera, and most importantly, The Virginian. The soap operas, and shows like The Virginian, had as high as a 94 percent viewership, according to regular news reports.

Nilva charged them ten cents each to watch from outside one of their windows and fifty cents from inside if it was raining. She hoped that the money she earned from her little TV business would make it so she wouldn't have to go back to digging for tin cans.

At the age of thirteen, she made arrangements to get a work permit, even though the legal limit was fourteen, and started working full-time, as well as going to school. The next six years she worked and studied and was able to rent a house for her and her mother in a better area. Her sister had moved out by this point. The next step for her was a huge one. She went to a car dealer and showed her skills by selling herself as a car salesperson even though she didn't have any experience. However, Nilva learned quickly and paid attention. She and others may not have recognized it as first, but she was a natural salesperson with extraordinary skill and the ability through sincerity and truthfulness to have people believe what she was telling them. She studied everything she could about what was going on to help her move forward. From fishing, she learned that the person who catches the most fish is the one who lets the fish take the bait before pulling the rod.

Nilva always looked for opportunities to refine her skills. One time she challenged her fellow salespeople at the car dealership to see who could sell the most cars in one day. She believed she could sell three in one day.

"Three! Three! Are you kidding me? How could anyone sell that many cars in a day?" her coworkers asked her in disbelief. But Nilva used the principles she had learned in collecting and selling tin cans and left the sales manager with his jaw dangling.

Incredible sales happened frequently with her. A normal month for her was anywhere from twenty-four to thirty-two cars but some months were spectacular. The other salespeople, jealous of her success, tried unsuccessfully to demean her efforts. The man who had previously been the top salesperson made some very brutal, unkind remarks one day in a sales meeting. She grabbed a telephone off a nearby desk and threw it so hard it broke his nose. That ended any unkind criticism from him. And her sales record solidified her as one to be respected.

Nilva in Brazil.

When salespeople asked to accompany her on a sales call to see how she did it, they were shocked to see how much dedication and effort went into being the top salesperson. They were stunned when she told them to be ready to go at two a.m. "Two a.m., are you off your rocker?" they would say. But she would respond, "If you want to sell cars, you have to be ready when they're ready."

This particular sales call was at a large security company and the only time the employees had available was from two to five a.m. Nilva didn't even blink twice. If you want to catch fish, you have to go where they are when they're there.

She was recognized for her ingenuity in opening doors previously shut. With her success came recognition and prosperity. She bought a large, exclusive piece of property just outside the city, but not too far from her work. She had an engineer design a beautiful house for her in a gated community that was on par with the best of those in São Paulo. To top it all off, she contacted one of the directors of Telefonica, the largest national phone company, convincing him to let her present her program for purchasing cars to the employees. To say it was a great success is putting it mildly. She sold more than five hundred cars to that one company.

As with many things in her life, Nilva had some very difficult trials yet to go through. One day not far from her office, three men ran up to her car as she was waiting in traffic for a stoplight to change. They banged on the windows with large caliber revolvers and demanded she open the doors. Once inside, she was repeatedly beaten by two of them while another robbed her purse and demanded she go with them to the nearest ATM machine to withdraw all her money. They told her once they got her money they were going to kill her.

She tried to reason with them, but they were like a pack of wild, brutal animals. Unbeknownst to them, a man in a car behind her had witnessed the whole encounter and had called the police on his cell phone. The man trailed behind the hijacked car and was in constant contact with the police. When the robbers opened the door and threw Nilva out while the vehicle was still moving, the police sprang into action. The police were swift and just as deadly as the attackers. The robbers were treated harshly to make sure they wouldn't harm anyone else.

As if that weren't enough, she was kidnapped again in less than a year with much the same outcome. Someone with a cell phone saw the attack and reported it. A blitz capture was undertaken and Nilva was set free.

I had a similar experience in the middle of São Paulo and know how dangerous a situation like this can be. In my case, there were two men on a motorcycle in heavy stop-and-go traffic. One of the men beat on my window with the barrel of his gun just inches from my face. He was screaming like a maniac, yelling that he wanted my wristwatch. If I didn't give it to him immediately, he would kill me. I didn't have to wonder long if he would have shot me had I not given him the watch. The next day the owner of a jewelry store was murdered in the same spot. I was thankful to be able to speak fluent Portuguese, and like Nilva, happy to know that daily prayer is an essential facet of my life.

When I brought her to the United States, she didn't let this foreign world hinder her progress or ambition. She learned to speak English fluently, became an American citizen, started her own very successful house cleaning business, and earned the equivalent of a college degree in practical business management—all a small part of what she's done in becoming the person her Father in Heaven wants her to be. She helps those that are sick and makes cakes for those that need cheering up on a daily basis.

And while I reside in a veteran's home to provide me with more intensive health care for the Parkinson's disease I've been suffering from for fifteen years, Nilva has sustained a home and ran her house cleaning business. She has cleaned as many as four houses per day, gone home, and nearly passed out from exhaustion just to get up the next day and do it all over again. This little badly burned girl has overcome many obstacles and will yet register many more victories. No doubt these things influenced her outlook, personality, desire, and determination for success and peace.

LOST OVER THE AMAZON

AMAZON

I was once seated near the front of an airplane on my way to Phoenix, which meant that I was one of the first ones to feel the blast of heat from the Arizona sunshine as the stewardess opened the door for exiting. The idea crossed my mind that maybe it was time to consider some sincere repentance because this kind of heat couldn't be normal. I reflected back on that experience as I entered the Amazon. I had no concept of what the Amazon was like the first time I ventured into it. As I found out, it was like Phoenix, except with humidity. Although I had found the climate brutal, I had also discovered they were producing at least five thousand carats of diamonds per week. It was hot, humid, uncomfortable, and dangerous. But I was about to take control of a large portion of the production of diamonds in that area, so I justified the misery.

I had previously had some experience with diamonds in Sierra Leone; however, I had not ventured much further into the industry because of the difficulty of doing business in West Africa. However, I had done a little business with diamonds in Brazil. Nevertheless, I received an interesting phone call one day from a man who had been buying and selling diamonds in the Amazon. He said he lived on the northern coast of Brazil. He had a good business and a nice family, and he didn't want to get shot or scalped for being greedy. So he told me that after confronting millions of bugs, huge snakes of all kinds, wild animals, and Indians that made the jaguars look tame, he just wanted to be back home in an environment where he could be happy and safe.

I asked him why he thought I would be interested in such a project, seeing as it hadn't treated him that well. He told me that he had met some people that had done business with me in Minas Gerais. They had told him they trusted me completely to sell anything. That was a pretty big compliment because we were talking about a lot of money. He said he had several thousand carats of diamonds. He would fly down to Salvador in the state of Bahia and give me the stones to sell for him. "You're barking up the wrong tree," I told him. I didn't have enough knowledge to take someone else's diamonds and sell them in a foreign market. Nevertheless, he had called me because he knew he could trust me. He said he had every confidence in me, which had been instilled in him by a company that he and some others were dealing with. They actually knew quite a bit about me. They knew I had gemstone offices in Brazil, the United States, Belgium, Germany, Korea, Hong Kong, and Bangkok. He said that anyone who could do business in that many places could surely find a place to do business with these diamonds. I asked him specifically what he wanted to do. He told me to sell the diamonds anywhere I wanted, get the best price, and give him a percentage of the deal.

He chuckled as I stammered and stuttered, but he assured me that it would be all right. He trusted me, and he knew that I would bring him his money along with my own profit. I felt flattered, but overwhelmed. I inquired of him when he wanted to begin and where I could get the diamonds. He replied that he would be on a flight to Salvador that afternoon, and he would give me the merchandise at the airport.

As agreed upon, I met him on the tarmac. I saw a man wearing a white shirt and dark pants. He wasn't carrying any bags, so I assumed this was my guy. He asked if I was Wayne, knowing it was because being Caucasian tends to give me away in such matters. I confirmed that I was Wayne and he swiftly took a couple thousand carats of diamonds out of the pocket of his pants, gave them to me, turned around, and was back on the plane in less than a minute.

Now, as great as this opportunity was, it just so happened that this was a time when getting into the diamond business for a low capital investment anywhere in the world was not really feasible. I had to get some help from someone for selling the goods and cutting the diamonds. The cost of labor for diamond cutters was very high in Europe but very low in India. I spent a number of days going from door to door to find someone who would do it all for cheap. In the end, I had to travel to Antwerp, Belgium.

During my stay in Antwerp, I met a man who owned a diamond reporting business. They surveyed and reported on the weekly diamond prices and how much people paid for all different sizes, colors, and cuts of stones. It was obvious to me that a man with these qualifications was exactly what I needed right then. We went out to dinner where he informed me that he would be happy to let me use his office in Antwerp, as I had hoped. He was actually excited to help me sell my goods, to mentor me in the business. It would give him more firsthand information about what was happening in the market that he couldn't otherwise get. My mentor helped me make the sales, selling the diamonds to stonecutters, primarily ones in Antwerp.

I was thrilled to have found my way into the market so quickly, especially since I didn't even have any money to get myself started. But I knew that if I weren't careful about how I did things, I would lose the little money I did have. I made it back to Brazil without problems. I called the man whose gemstones I had sold to give him the good news. He was so excited that he could hardly talk. He informed me that he had just received word that there was a huge lot of many thousands of carats of diamonds waiting for somebody to buy. Things were going pretty fast. I felt a little distinctive voice warning me to be careful. But I had just stepped into this business in a remarkable fashion. And now there were tens of thousands of carats available for the picking. That was the problem; I was getting greedy.

The challenge, then, was to get back to the Amazon as fast as possible and leverage as much money and as many carats of diamonds as I could. I didn't know how to grade the diamonds, which meant I didn't know how long I needed to do my end of things. But I did know that deals like this didn't last long. In order to get where I was going in the Amazon basin, I had to fly from Salvador to Brasilia and then from Brasilia to Cuiabá. Then I had to charter a small plane to escort me on a three and a half-hour trip over the jungle to get to the area where the diamonds were. The thing is, when you're traveling in the gemstone business, you make it a rule never to talk to anybody. You don't want them to know anything, even though you've got this fantastic story burning a hole in your pocket.

When I got to the airport at Cuiabá, I realized that I was a little too late. Every single plane had been chartered. I was frantic to get to those diamonds before somebody else did. Conveniently, I found two other men who were going to the same place. Together, the three of us were able to find a plane. But then we couldn't find a pilot. We finally found a little spit-behind-the-ears kid. He didn't have much experience, but the man with the plane assured us that the boy had just graduated from aeronautical school, so he had all the latest background and training that anyone would need.

None of us felt comfortable having a novice fly us to our destination, but everybody had the same desire to get to Juína. These other two men had also heard about the diamonds, so we all discussed the risk and reward of getting there before other buyers showed up, despite the competition we felt toward each other. As I weighed the pros and cons of getting into this plane with a novice pilot, greed won out that day.

One of the men had a new type of GPS-based tracking unit that contained an electronic compass. He assured us that even though there was no Omni gear in the Amazon, all we had to do was set the proper degree, and it would take us right to the spot where we wanted to go. The pilot, though, decided to use his own compass as well.

The takeoff went pretty smoothly, and I felt some degree of optimism. I had flown this way many times before with good, experienced pilots, so I knew the way pretty well. I had once discovered that you could pretty well figure out the direction you are going by using the bends in some of the rivers below. During the first ten or fifteen minutes of this flight, I noticed that the jungle had been deforested. The pilot was using his compass and trying to compare it to the man's GPS, which had given the pilot some coordinates. He started acting like a kid with a new toy. As we went farther, I began to have trouble recognizing any of the area that we were flying over.

Time went by. We were flying a route that these two whizzos had come up with on their directional instruments. I had learned to recognize some geographical landmarks during previous trips, but I didn't recognize any at this point. I voiced my concern to the pilot. The initial smart aleck remarks were now replaced by some degree of concern. The other man complained loudly and even began to threaten the pilot. But we continued on and on. Still there were no recognizable landmarks of any kind. Finally we realized the truth with great concern: we were lost!

The pilot suggested that we begin circling to see if we could spot a road or an area where the forest had been cleared off. One of the men called everyone's attention to the two fuel gauges, which were both very low. Between the low fuel and the approaching twilight, the situation became grave. The man beside me told the pilot that if he didn't find a spot for us to land, he would throw him out of the plane. Some comfort that was. Even though this doofus was the one flying the plane, it was better than having no pilot at all.

Every minute seemed like a lifetime by now. Both tank gauges were nearly on empty, and darkness was fast approaching. My three fellow passengers, who must have been Catholic, kept crossing themselves. I remembered right then a flight that I had been on to go from Panama to La Paz, Bolivia. At the time, I spoke very little Spanish. But when the pilot made an announcement over the loudspeaker and smoke started coming out of the left wing, people were crying and kneeling on the floor in prayer. And I didn't really have to know much Spanish to understand that things weren't too good. We had fortunately made it back to Panama where the plane was repaired as all the passengers sat looking out the window. I had continually wondered when they would take us off the aircraft, hoping it would be before it exploded. In less than half an hour, the mechanics began high-fiving each other with big smiles on their faces. They closed the door, and away we went.

Because I have traveled extensively for fifteen years all over the world, there have been a lot of adventures in flying. But being lost above the Amazon with no fuel was in a category all on its own. I could see my life fading away by the minute. The threats, the insults, and the desperation of the furious passenger had now turned to prayer. At the time, I was trying to figure out why the man was so vicious and threatening. I figured he was simply greedy, like me. . . .

All of the sudden, everybody looked out the windows on the left side of the plane, letting out cries of joy. There was a road below us! It probably wasn't wide enough to land a plane on, but it was a road. Being this deep in the jungle, it was probably for people who hauled timber. Our tanks were dangerously low, so we needed a place to land the plane.

Hallelujah! There was an opening in a lumber camp. They had a crude airstrip. Our hearts jumped for joy! From their comments, it appeared that my companions didn't have any more confidence in this pilot's landing ability than in his ability to guide and direct the plane. The pilot aimed directly for the end of the landing strip. As we approached the strip, we realized that it obviously wasn't very long. The pilot dropped that plane so fast and so hard that it bounced at least twenty feet back in the air! He had hit the ground at an angle, and for a moment, it looked like we were going to run into the timber cutters' cabins. It took two or three more jumps before the plane finally settled down on the runway. The manager of the operation approached us once we were stopped and said with a chuckle, "Will you be wanting to stay with us tonight?"

We all let out a deep sigh of relief as they greeted us and showed us to the rustic but surprisingly comfortable cabins. I was delighted to see how well we were treated. They served us a delicious hot meal. They told us that we could manually pump fuel from the drums that they had there so we could get to where we were supposed to go. As it turned out, the timber operation was further away from our destination of Juína than we had been when we started. I learned right then that the longer you follow the wrong trajectory, the more off course you will be.

After dinner, I decided to take some time for myself. I wandered off to the edge of the forest and sat down to reflect on the events of the day. I understood then that the thing that had triggered this nearly disastrous flight was the greed that I nurtured when I heard about how many diamonds were going to be available. I thanked my Father in Heaven for his deliverance, for giving me another chance to change my life and habits for the better. Most experiences in life are not quite as dramatic as this one had been, but it was surely one that I would not soon forget. I was down to just a few last minutes. I would have forfeited my life for a few little shiny stones.

I sat there pondering for a while before going back to the loggers' camp. They were very courteous to us. They shared a few stories about people missing their guideposts and crashing. There had even been one commercial jet that got caught in the same situation. The pilot had circled around until he had run out of fuel. The plane ended up crashing. If I recall correctly, the majority of the passengers perished. That night, I fell asleep quickly due to immense exhaustion, but I was tormented by dreams of a falling aircraft.

The next morning, we started early with an excellent breakfast. The foreman of the lumber camp sat at the same table as us. The pilot worked out a payment for the fuel he would need to get us to our destination. The pilot started talking about the route he was going to take to fly us to

Juína. Although all three of us were paying for the trip, there immediately began to be protests and the malicious man, Mario, began to curse and threaten the pilot. The foreman settled things down and explained that if we followed the river that was on the edge of the runway, it would take us directly from where we currently were to Juína. He said there was no way to get lost as long as we followed the river.

Mario took this as an opportunity to let the pilot know that he was in more peril from the passengers than anything if he took his plane off course again. He also told him that if there were any problems at all, he would teach him how to fly—without an airplane. After that, I didn't think I could add anything else to what had already been said, so I remained quiet and kept a firm grip on the map that the lumbermen gave me.

The pilot was very jittery, but the takeoff got us in the air, although it only cleared the trees by about ten feet. According to the instructions from the lumbermen, and by the markings on the map, following the river was pretty simple. It took a couple of hours to get there. But at least this time, there was a landing strip. Everybody hung on for dear life as this whiz-bang pilot hit hard and bounced again. We had two or three more hops before we finally settled on the ground. What a relief! I didn't know where I could find another charter plane back to Cuiabá, but I knew it wouldn't be with this guy.

Well, it was a hectic couple of days in the jungle, and the buying competition was fierce. There were large quantities of diamonds available from numerous miners. I was very happy with the lots I had purchased. When the company that owned the plane, along with everyone else in Juína, heard about the lack of proficiency of our pilot, they sent an experienced pilot to take his place. I was fortunate enough to catch a commercial flight with a twelve-passenger capacity. It felt like a deluxe 747 compared to the other one that had nearly sealed my doom. For Mario, on the other hand, fate took a different route. He is presently serving a twenty-two-year sentence in a federal penitentiary in Brazil for murder and hijacking.

And how was your day at the office?

RED DIAMOND

AMAZON

During the early to mid-eighties, I became more interested and involved in the diamond business. The challenge was I knew very little about diamonds. From my viewpoint it was a very information-demanding type of business.

I bought books, took classes, and thoroughly immersed myself in the diamond trade. It all pretty much came down to this: Did I buy at a low enough price to make a profit? I bought a large quantity of diamonds over the years, but there was one particular stone I'm sure I'll never forget.

There is sameness among diamonds that can be very deceptive if you don't know what you're looking for. To the untrained eye, one diamond could cost a fraction of the price of another seemingly similar diamond. Diamonds are evaluated by five major factors:

1. Shape
2. Carat
3. Cut
4. Color
5. Clarity

These factors can, and frequently do, change the diamond's relational value. By this time, I had been in the diamond business long enough to have an understanding of not only what factors were presently influencing the market, but how that change of one item could influence the others. In the area of Mato Grosso where I was mining, it was not uncommon to find brown, pink, green, and other colors with relatively high values.

However, due to the shape and defects that were often characteristic of the stones, they didn't command very high prices.

With these factors in mind, my buying expertise was really put to the test one day as I was walking along a jungle trail to find the owner of a mine that produced good quality, clean stones. I didn't find him, but I did find another dealer whom I had known for a long time from Minas Gerais. He seemed to be in a hurry and told me he wanted to get out of the jungle where he could make a deal on the goods he had just purchased. He offered me the lot, as he opened the paper to reveal three red stones. I was dumbfounded. There, like three little Easter eggs were the cleanest, most beautiful, sparkling, blood red stones I had ever seen. The largest was about 1.5 carats, and the two smaller stones were about half that size. The problem was I didn't know what they were. One could reason from the circumstances they could only be diamonds, but I didn't have any knowledge whatsoever about red diamonds. The largest of the stones was a work of art, regardless of what kind of stone it was.

He wanted fifty thousand dollars for the lot and would not sell for a penny less. He was in a hurry and didn't want to waste time talking. While those were good signs to a buyer, that was still a lot of money. There were no phones in the jungle, so I hurried back to Juína and on to Cuiabá where I called my associate in Antwerp. He went just about nuts and told me to get back on the plane and find the seller right now. He told me if I needed the money in my bank account, he would put it in immediately. What he emphasized was to find the seller as quickly as possible.

Well, after tracking him all night, I found the dealer at his home in Belo Horizonte early the next morning. He had sold the stones the night before for forty-two thousand dollars. I was really disappointed, but knew I had given it my best try.

Months later I was in Antwerp and went to my associate's office. He handed me a weekly trade journal and said he was going to ruin my day. I opened the book to where he indicated and saw that the red stone had been cut down to ninety-three carats (.93) and had sold at an auction for $880,000.

Have you ever been kicked in the stomach by a wild bull?

NEEDLE IN THE HAYSTACK

I don't know how many members of the Church of Jesus Christ of Latter-day Saints there were in Mexico City in 1976, but the city had a total population of approximately eight million people.[1] That means your odds of simply happening upon a familiar face are terrible. Let me explain.

A couple of friends and I had driven to Mexico to meet a few more friends. We planned to explore some roads and artifacts that we had been studying for some time. In case you haven't driven from the United States to the heart of Mexico, let me tell you that it's a very long drive. For us it was a non-stop sixty-hour trip. We drove a big station wagon to be more comfortable—but it was still a long way.

We spent a couple of weeks traveling around Mexico with our companions whom we had met up with. Eventually we parted company with them and drove on to Mexico City. It was two or three o'clock in the morning when we arrived. Since it was a Saturday night, and we wanted to go to church the next morning, we knew we'd end up spending only a few hours in a hotel room. In those days, we were students and on a very meager budget, so as we got closer to Mexico City and as it grew later and later, we thought it best to conserve our funds and sleep in the car. The question was where. Mexico City was well known for danger outside of the populated, well-lit areas.

As we discussed it, we decided to drive around the safe, residential areas and park our car in front of a nice-looking house. We knew the police patrolled residential areas and would give us a hard time if they found us, but we were so exhausted we decided to try. We saw quite a few police as we looked for a parking place, but seeing them comforted us. With so many dangerous people infesting the streets of Mexico City at night, we probably looked like harmless school kids to the Mexican police.

After extensive searching, we found a street or two that looked and felt good to us, but for some reason we kept looking. We were generally looking for a place without movement or extra lights so we could stay fairly hidden. We meandered through a few more streets, ending up at the first one we had considered. We offered a prayer and were drawn immediately to one particular house. There wasn't a lot of discussion. We simply pulled up on the street, which sat across a series of bare fields, covered up, and fell asleep immediately.

We were awakened to the sound of a car pulling out of the driveway past us. The car was full of people dressed for church. They were all pointing at us. We had no idea who they were or what they might be saying to each other, but the next thing we saw gladdened our hearts and left us amazed: the car had Utah license plates on it. We didn't know who they were, but we reasoned they were church members. We followed them for a half hour, and sure enough there was a chapel standing like a beacon of light on a foggy coast.

We got out of the car, hoping and praying that no one who saw us would be alarmed at what a sorry-looking bunch we were. But when we entered the chapel, we were received warmly and even asked to teach the lesson for the priesthood quorum. It was a wonderful experience.

We met the family who owned the house we'd slept in front of the night before, and they were delightful and friendly. The mother invited us over for dinner and told us we could shower, if we wanted. That was a welcome invitation, and we immediately accepted. When we asked what they were doing in Mexico, we found that the mother of the family was the niece of Elder Bruce R. McConkie, one of the Apostles of the LDS church. We reflected back to our humble prayer the night before and the amazing blessings that had followed.

I've reflected on that trip many times over the years. If you look at it from the viewpoint of probability, it would have been absolutely improbable to find a safe place to park, a beautiful Latter-day Saint family, and a way to the church without the guidance of the Spirit. Yet, by trusting the Spirit, we were led right to where we needed to be. Experiences like this have added to my testimony bit by bit, like small oil drops dripping into a lantern and building up throughout my life.

NOTES

1.   See   https://www.google.com/publicdata/explore?ds=z83fj27m8fa7gq_&met_y=po pulation&idim=state:DF&hl=en&dl=en.

THE MAN IN THE ROAD

BAHIA, BRAZIL

Sunday afternoon is a time for resting, which often means rolling over and catching another twenty winks. And in Bahia, a northeastern state of Brazil, people are famous for being nearly comatose on Sunday afternoons.

It was that kind of afternoon as I rested with two American families who were in Brazil to adopt children. I was helping them because I knew the area very well and I spoke the language fluently. When I first mentioned I was going to help some families adopt, my Brazilian associates told me I would never be able to do it. They said the Brazilian people are very jealous because these children would have a better life than they did. I scoffed at such foolish and wicked ideas, but these observances were very prophetic—it turns out I was the naïve one.

Not only is Bahia famous for being laid-back, but I was in a particularly peaceful setting I knew very well. It was a beautiful day and I was sitting in the shade of some palm trees near the swimming pool. I had been in Alagoinhas earlier in the morning to take two couples and the three children they were looking to adopt to our church meetings. The morning went very well. I couldn't have programmed it to go any better than it did. The children were all happy and they fit in with the other children at church. After church one couple stayed in Alagoinhas and the other came back to Feira de Santana with me. We hadn't been back that long from the church meetings and everybody had eaten a nice dinner.

Yet notwithstanding the peaceful setting, I felt restless. I felt more and more agitated as time went by. I had this awful feeling in the pit of my stomach and as I meditated, trying to find an answer to what was causing my agitation, the feeling only got worse. My thoughts were a mixture of fear, danger, and restlessness. I'd had other such feelings before, but they had been promptings to warn me in certain dangerous situations that I occasionally encountered in the backcountry of South America.

The more I thought about it, the more it seemed like someone was calling me. The wooden shuttered windows were open, letting the breeze blow through my open-air home. The couple was watching the child play on the floor. Everyone was relaxed and enjoying themselves but me. I felt like a Mexican jumping bean. There were no visible problems and nothing I could discern that would have caused trouble. As I meditated, it became clear to me there was someone with a problem somewhere that needed help.

I have found from personal experience that when you obey a prompting, especially when you don't know exactly what it is, the Lord finds a way to provide for your needs or the needs of those that stand in want. I stood up and announced that I was going back to Alagoinhas. I didn't know if there was a problem in Alagoinhas, but I knew I had to go. The couple wasn't really too sure they wanted to make that trip again because it was a difficult road with lots of potholes. Although I knew it would be safer for them to stay with me, I knew I had to go whether they came or not. Experience and wise people have taught me to follow promptings.

I suppose the couple thought it was better to go for a joy ride with me than to stay somewhere they didn't speak the language. I prodded them along to the car as I felt a greater urgency to leave every minute. I was practically in a panic by the time I got the car going. I pulled out of the area where I lived, on the outskirts of town, and followed the traffic circle. This took me to the highway that led to Alagoinhas and Salvador.

We hadn't gone more than a quarter mile when our chit chat—which had distracted me from my driving—nearly caused us a catastrophe. We were leaving the city and everyone was driving fast, jockeying to get a spot in the flow of traffic. Suddenly, there appeared a man in front of me in the traffic lanes. I pulled the wheel hard to keep from hitting him. It looked as though he was trying to get someone to run him over. I felt sick and shocked as I looked at the situation. Cars were swerving around the man, ensuring that traffic didn't slowed down at all. I tried to get over to the right to get out of the traffic flow and to help the man who was obviously trying to commit suicide. There was a traffic circle immediately ahead. I went straight for the inside of that so as to ensure missing the other drivers and getting back in the return lane so I could get back to help the man in traffic.

The man was tall and had dark curly hair and a beard. He was shirtless without shoes and was dressed only in denim pants. He was walking back and forth across the lanes of traffic, eyes cast down to the ground. Apparently he didn't want to see his own death; he wanted it to be a surprise. I had seen this same thing often in Mexico City. Over a period of two or three years, I don't remember one visit when I didn't see somebody walking in traffic trying to end this earthly misery.

The distraction the man was causing in the swift-moving traffic snarled up the road with horns honking and people shouting. I finally got through traffic and headed back around the traffic circle to get where the man was. Right as I came into the circle there was a police unit there with a pickup truck that had five or six armed police in it. I pulled up next to the truck and shouted to the driver that there was a man trying to kill himself up the road. The officer said he would follow me. I pulled off the road near the man who was in the middle of the multilane highway, knowing that I needed to use some caution so as to not push him more over the edge than he already was. I jumped out of my car while it was still slightly rolling, pulling the emergency break on my way out. I tried getting the man's attention but he wouldn't look away from the ground. He wouldn't be distracted by anything. He seemed resolute in his mission of getting himself run over.

As I walked onto the road, toward the man, traffic began to slow a little. I realized that the people didn't know if this was a single or double suicide when they saw me on the road. I approached the man cautiously, being careful to not startle him or make him fearful. I had to be very careful; both of our lives were on the line now. The cars were shooting by us as I carefully eased my way closer, keeping one eye on him and the other on the traffic. I had a terrific surge of adrenaline as I neared the man. I stuck out my hand and put it on his arm. I said to him, "You don't have to do this. It's all right. Let's get out of the traffic and talk it over."

Without looking up, he spoke softly but with incredible emotion. It actually brought tears to my eyes. He said, "Nobody loves me." Still without looking up, he slowly shook his head and said, "No."

Although his words were resistant, his body was not. He was sobbing and docile as I gently led him off to the side of the road.

One of the police came over and said to me and the other police gathered around, "I know this man. He's a good man. I don't know why he's doing this, but he's a good responsible man, and I guess he's just been deeply hurt by something." The policeman showed a lot of sympathy and gentleness, which the police in that city are not famous for.

And then all the emotion in the man came to the surface in one big rush. He was sobbing and crying uncontrollably. It was really a painful sight to see somebody hurting so much emotionally, to see someone suffering like that. I felt much better when I saw several police and people from the neighborhood that had gathered by this time speak soothing words to him and walk him toward his home, which was just off the side of the highway.

I knew one thing for sure: if ever I am prompted to do something, even if it's something I don't want to do, I need to just readjust my priorities and do as the Spirit prompts. This experience made me remember the times when I heeded promptings, from turning off a highway to walking down an alternate street. The Lord can bless us if we make ourselves available and reach out to those in need mentally, physically, and spiritually.

And it turns out that my Brazilian associates were right; the adoptions didn't go through. The police were even sent after me because I had apparently upset their scheme of milking money from these American couples who were there to adopt children.

BETWEEN THE POLES

UTAH / NEVADA BORDER

For those of you who don't know Dale Tingey, you'd be in for quite an experience. Whether at a pulpit addressing hundreds of people or at a Havasupai village in the bottom of the Grand Canyon, he is hard to forget.

Dale is most beloved for his great long-term work and kindness. While serving as Director of Indian Affairs at Brigham Young University for several decades, Dale became one of the most prominent members of the LDS Church in its relationship with the Native Americans of North and Central America. He'd receive assignments directly from General Authorities of the LDS Church, and off he would go in his little plane, flying to remote places all over the country and often landing on unknown roads and other flat spots that looked available from above.

He once remarked that the General Authorities recommended he stop flying his well-worn plane to such remote locations, as it was "much too dangerous." But in the next breath they would hand him a schedule to visit a number of far-off tribes or leaders of tribes, each location calibrated perfectly to fit into a small travel agenda. He said that the only way to fulfill each assignment was to fly his plane. In one General Conference, a General Authority spoke of flying with Dale. He remarked how frightened he was—he thought airplanes were supposed to fly over power lines, but Dale had occasion to fly under them!

Dale had his own aircraft for many years. It was a Cessna CCX. Yet, the remarkable thing was not the plane, but the pilot. Each newcomer would get initiated with Dale's version of "Rock-a-bye Baby." It's easy to guess what happened when he'd sing "And down will come baby, cradle and all." Let me tell you, it wasn't for the faint of heart. A vertical dive in a plane that Orville and Wilbur Wright passed over when they were looking for spare parts is unique, to say the least. He would sure take you for a wild ride.

Before flight, Dale always paused to have a word of prayer. If you didn't feel the need for it before the flight, you always did before touching ground again. Many cross themselves during a flight—even if they're not Catholic.

I always admired Dale, but it was on one particular trip that I grew to respect his humility and his expertise in flying planes. Dale and I were with a mutual friend also named Dale. We were headed north and passed over a place called Koosharem in Utah, which had a population of 276. As we flew, a tremendous black cloud blocked our way, and we had to fly west to avoid the ensuing storm. The original plan had been to go to Richfield and follow the highway to Provo, but the storm was approaching so fast that we had to go almost due west.

We started looking for any kind of road where we could take the plane down. The storm was so strong, black, and packed with moisture that ice forming on the wings became a real concern. Dale was trying to get around the storm, but it was moving so fast that we couldn't find a place to land the plane. We were soon flying just several hundred feet off the ground.

We had flown quite a ways west and were on the borderline of Nevada, near a range of mountains that ran north and south. Dale had considered going over the mountains and landing in Ely, Nevada, but a fierce wind was blowing off the mountain, preventing him from elevating the plane. Thankfully, we found a dirt road and followed it to see if we could find shelter at a farmhouse. Though our situation looked grim, we eventually saw lights shining from a farmhouse at the end of the road. Dale had the plane very close to the ground and battled the wind by flying at an angle to the road.

The road was oriented toward the mountains, and a row of power lines lined the east side of it. Because of the strength of the wind coming off the hills, the power lines worried us. If a gust of wind caught us as we tried to land, we could crash into the poles of the power lines.

And that's almost what happened. As we neared the ground, a gust of wind caught the plane and blew us off to the right toward two poles. We barely passed through the opening between them. Only the Lord's mercy and Dale's expertise as a pilot saved us. Dale pulled the plane back up in the air and circled around to attempt another landing—only to have another near-death experience.

The wind was so strong that we were flying nearly sideways. With all three of us engaged in mighty prayer, Dale lined up for another try at getting the plane on the ground. Dale had been a fighter pilot instructor in World War II and had been known to fly through the arches of southern Utah, and our lives now depended on the next second's reaction and skill gained from his experiences. With gale force winds still blowing us sideways, he miraculously worked the controls to whip the plane into a straight line just as we hit the ground, immediately shooting left toward brush and a wood fence. Dale quickly corrected it and got us back on the road. We were anxious to get the plane secured and escape the bitter, freezing wind.

As we climbed out of the plane, two pickup trucks pulled up, to our relief. When we saw the drivers, we felt like we had flown into a time tunnel and back to the 1800s. Two cowboys stepped out of their trucks, but didn't walk toward us. They both had pistols strapped to their waists and stood watching us cautiously. Eventually we asked if they had any rope, they brought it over, and we got the plane secured to the corrals.

The cowboys, who were brothers, said they had been having some trouble with a few outlaws from the Ely area that had been rustling their cattle. It was rough, wide open country. After conversing with each other out of our earshot, they invited us to have dinner and to spend the night with them. They were pretty crusty on the outside and their language was rather crude, but they were good men and saved us in a difficult circumstance. One brother told us it was a good thing we had chosen to avoid flying over to Ely. The last plane to try it in this kind of weather, he said, was still up there—in pieces.

After a nice dinner prepared by their wives, the cowboys provided us with warm bedding and old-fashioned hospitality. Dale stayed with one brother, and the other Dale and I stayed with the other. We enjoyed a good night's sleep and a nice breakfast the next morning. We learned from our discussion that the brothers had been baptized into the LDS Church long ago, and although they smoked and drank coffee, they were good men and very compassionate to us. They were evidence that charity never faileth!

After breakfast, we verified that everything was all right with the plane and thanked them. As the plane lifted off the ground, we felt very grateful for the calm, peaceful air that lifted us up toward the clouds. Dale wiggled the wings back and forth to wave goodbye to our newfound friends. We passed through Ely so Dale could take care of his church duties and then sailed through clear skies back to Provo.

Over the years, I've been very grateful for having been in the presence of a man of Dale's humble character in perilous times and circumstances. Being around him has given me a desire to be a better person. We had many other flights and adventures, all of them very memorable to me.

Wayne in Tahiti.

FINAL THOUGHTS

My hope by sharing these life stories is that readers will gain an understanding of the unknown, whether that be far off places or unfamiliar circumstances.

I hope they learn they can't be afraid to fail—you must have the courage to try or you have failed already. I hope that all who read this, including my four sons and their families, will never be afraid to fail. Go for what's right. Go for the gold.

And finally, through life's experiences, you must come to learn who you are—that is the greatest of all life's lessons and rewards.

Wayne at the VA home.

ABOUT THE AUTHOR

After graduating from Brigham Young University in 1976 with a bachelor's in communications with an emphasis in journalism, Wayne Hamby traveled to faraway lands where he spent most of his life doing business in the distant jungles and mist-shrouded mountains. Wayne has since relocated to Payson, Utah, where he is sort of retired, but busier than ever writing about his adventures.

www.waynehamby.com